THE DRAMA OF THE APOCALYPSE

THE DRAMA OF THE APOCALYPSE

IN RELATION TO THE LITERARY AND
POLITICAL CIRCUMSTANCES
OF ITS TIME

BY

FREDERIC PALMER

AUTHOR OF "STUDIES IN THEOLOGIC DEFINITION"

New York
THE MACMILLAN COMPANY
LONDON: MACMILLAN & CO., Ltd.
1903

All rights reserved

COPYRIGHT, 1903,
By THE MACMILLAN COMPANY.

Set up and electrotyped May, 1903.

Norwood Press
J. S. Cushing & Co. — Berwick & Smith Co.
Norwood, Mass., U.S.A.

CONTENTS

	PAGE
PREFACE	vii

CHAPTER		
I.	THE DRAMATIC CHARACTER OF THE APOCALYPSE	1
II.	SIGNS OF THE TIMES	22
III.	THE DRAMA	35
IV.	THE END OF ALL THINGS	87
V.	THE PERSON OF JESUS	98
VI.	THE LITERARY VALUE OF THE APOCALYPSE	113
VII.	THE BOOK OF THE REVELATION	122
APPENDIX		191

PREFACE

The following Study of the Apocalypse is intended to be not so much a critical examination as an appreciation. It does not aim to be a commentary, a museum of research, nor an embodiment of decisions upon the many scholastic questions involved. It endeavors rather to invite, and to smooth the way before the ordinary reader. There is lying ready much piety which would gladly find fresh food, much literary appreciation which would welcome a new masterpiece, much poetic sensibility waiting to test fire by itself. Too often when one of these has approached the Book of the Revelation it has been repelled by language it could not understand. But for all these classes the Book is peculiarly an inheritance. It needs but a little to put them in possession of their own. That little this Essay is ambitious to accomplish.

One of the first principles of the Biblical Study of our day is that we cannot know what the Bible means for us until we know something of what it meant for those to whom it was uttered. It is in accordance with this principle that in coming to the Apocalypse we seek first to find what it meant to the Christian of the latter half of the first century. Its value for us may not be the same as for him, but it will be on the same lines. The spiritual lessons will be similar, though the circumstances through which they are taught may be different. It is this conviction of the necessity of penetrating through its outer circumstances to a knowledge of the mind of the time, that has led to the present Study of the Apocalypse.

F. P.

ANDOVER, MASS.

"And the Apocalypse of St. John is the majestic image of a high and stately tragedy, shutting up and intermingling her solemn scenes and acts with a sevenfold chorus of hallelujahs and harping symphonies."

— JOHN MILTON, "The Reason of Church Government."

"The soul has said, 'I do not know what all these emblems, in which angels and devils and beasts with heads and horns are introduced, may exactly signify, but I do see that all brute-power will be overcome by holy love; I do see that all vain cunning will be proved to be vain by holy wisdom; I do see that the Lord of the great heavens will, governing here as well as on high, and managing His transactions according to great preparations made in the invisible scene, bear down with helpful powers upon the earth, and make the changes below correspond to the changes above.'"

— FREDERICK D. MAURICE, "Lectures on the Apocalypse."

THE DRAMA OF THE APOCALYPSE

CHAPTER I

THE DRAMATIC CHARACTER OF THE APOCALYPSE

THE Revelation of St. John is probably one of the least read and least valued of the books of the New Testament. The second and third chapters, the last, and parts of the twentieth and twenty-first stand, it is true, on a different plane in the mind of the ordinary reader, from the other parts of the Book. These speak a language as easily understood as that of the Gospels. The chapters which are supposed to be a description of Heaven have furnished a precious basis for the devout imagination in all ages. But the greater part of the Book is to most readers of the Bible a confused mass, into which angels and dragons and beasts with heads and horns, vials and trumpets, are introduced in no order and with no perceptible plan. And the ordinary reader is in one respect right. He can find what is better adapted to his purpose much more readily elsewhere. The value of the Book does not lie where he is accustomed to look for value, in texts, short quotable passages full of comfort or guidance or wisdom. It is a poetic value, requiring some power of literary appreciation to apprehend it. But when one comes to it with some degree of such capacity, the Book is found to be full of unity and force, of gorgeous coloring and majestic movement, full of those qualities of imagination which, when joined with the insight and judgment of a spiritual nature, give the power of inspiration. In many respects the Apocalypse is like that poem which owes so much to it, " Paradise Lost "; the excellences of both are to be sought in the same direction.

It is not a commentary, but a study of

materials, which is here aimed at in regard to the Apocalypse. What were the conditions of the mind of the time? What imprint was given to those conditions by the special characteristics of the author? What were the circumstances of the age which made a background for the writer's imagination? What the terms of time and place in which he set forth the eternal processes of the Kingdom of Heaven? Such a consideration of elements does not eliminate, but exhibits, the directly spiritual qualities — the power of reaching men's souls and bringing them into direct contact with the spirit of God — which the age contemporary with the Apocalypse recognized abundantly in it, which gave it a place in the Canon, and which have also been recognized, to some degree at least, by the ages since.

Like all Hebrew prophecy, the Apocalypse was designed by its author for the times in which he wrote, and had no intended application to future ages. Indeed, he did not contemplate the possibility that the world would last to future ages, for it was the object of his book to assure the Christian community that the end of the world would come in a very short time, a few years at the utmost. But like all Hebrew prophecy too, the author was dealing with facts and principles which were universal, and the words he uttered were too large to fit the immediate circumstances only. The future is really the same as the present; it is enfolded within it, and is governed by the same laws; and so what is true of the universal elements of the present, is true without limitation of time. This was expressed and strengthened to the mind of a Hebrew by the fact that his language had but two tenses, one for an action regarded as complete, whether present or past, the other for an action still incomplete, whether past, present, or future. A prophecy then which was true for its own time, was, because it dealt with universal elements, true for all time; but the form of it was that of its own day and conditions. It was uttered to meet present needs, and those present needs must be taken into account if the prophecy is to be understood either in its temporary or its permanent form.

The aim of the Apocalypse was to comfort and encourage the Christians of the latter part of the first century with the thought of the speedy end of the world and the establishment of the kingdom of their Lord. The clouds which for the present concealed Him from them were soon to roll back and He would be seen coming in glory, raising the dead, bringing punishment to the wicked and rewards to His faithful. The wonderful events which had been happening in the world of Nature and in that of politics were signs that His coming was at hand. There was apparently no part of the Christian belief which took so strong a hold on the imagination of those who had it, as this of the visible coming of Jesus to set up His kingdom in Jerusalem. His disciples were planning for it while they were with Him. Their first thought after His resurrection was that now it was to be accomplished.

We can trace the development of this belief in the mind of St. Paul. His earliest Epistle is partly an answer to questions about which the Thessalonian Church had apparently written to him. It indicates how little the doctrine of the resurrection was understood, that their difficulty was profound and widespread. The question was, Since the reward of the faithful would be to share in the kingdom Christ would establish, how about those who died before the establishment of the kingdom? Their fate seemed hard, for they would be debarred from their reward. But St. Paul says (1 Thess. iv. 13 f.) that he and the rest of them who will witness the coming of the Lord will have no advantage over those who had fallen asleep, for there will be a sudden shout by an archangel, and Jesus will descend from the sky and sit upon the clouds, and then the faithful who are dead will rise from their graves and be joined by the faithful who remain alive, and all together will ascend into the air and be forever with the Lord. And this great event may occur at any moment. This intelligence not unnaturally produced confusion in the Thessalonian Church. If the coming of the Lord might take place at any time, what was the use of carrying on longer one's ordinary business? It could not be needed if the world was to pass away soon. And so the members of the church fell into that disorder and antinomianism which the prospect of a speedy end of all things has always tended to produce. St. Paul therefore writes them again (2 Thess. ii. 3), telling them that the conditions of the Parousia are not fully ripe, and that whenever it may come, soon or late, they must abstain from lawlessness and anarchy and meet it walking soberly in the paths of ordinary life. But it is true, he assures them, the Lord will descend from Heaven with His mighty angels in flaming fire, bringing judgment and glory.

When now we turn to those Epistles of his which hold a middle place in date, we find that the details of the Lord's coming bear a less prominent part in them. The time is short, and one must not be entangled with the affairs of this life (1 Cor. vii. 29). The night is far spent; it is time to awake, for the day is at hand, and their salvation is nearer than when they entered the faith (Rom. xiii. 11, 12). They are to wait and keep blameless until the coming of the Lord Jesus Christ (1 Cor. i. 7, 8). But the reward of the faithful is now regarded not so much as rising into the sky to meet the Lord, as a spiritual change progressively into the likeness of Christ (2 Cor. iii. 18). And when we come to his latest Epistles we find that the circumstances of the Parousia are hardly mentioned, while its spiritual significance is brought still more fully into prominence. Our lower natures will be fashioned like the glorious body of Christ (Phil. iii. 20, 21). We shall be delivered from the power of darkness and made partakers of the inheritance of the saints in light (Col. i. 12, 13). Belief in the great fact of the coming of Christ still remains; "The Lord is at hand"(Phil. iv. 5); but its material dress has become of no importance. And at last the apostle sits in prison, an old man, having given up the expectation of himself beholding the coming of the Lord, but knowing that he shall depart and be with Christ, which after all is far better (2 Tim. iv. 6; Phil. i. 23).

This idea of the visible coming of the Lord entered most deeply into the mental atmosphere of Christian believers of the first century. It was to them what the conviction of the superiority of good over evil is to us, the centre of their faith, the source of their consolation and courage. Many centuries have shown the spiritual character of a belief in which to those who held it first, there was no separation between spiritual and material. And so it has come to pass that while to us the life of Christ marks the beginning of an era, to the early Christians it marked the end of one. This then was the aim of the Apocalypse, to assure them that their belief was correct; their triumph was sure and was at hand.

The Book is in the form of a drama. It

could hardly have had any other form, for the events it has to deal with are essentially dramatic, events which step by step inevitably bring about a final *dénoûment*. It is interesting to compare it with the other two dramas of classic Hebrew literature, the Book of Job and Solomon's Song; if, indeed, the Book of Job is Hebraic and not Idumean. Unlike Solomon's Song, which not improbably has been often represented at the marriages and feasts of the kings and nobles of Northern Israel, the Apocalypse can never have been intended for representation. Yet its stages or acts are marked by much greater precision than those of the older drama. When compared with the Book of Job, the changes which time had been working can be plainly seen. The Book of Job is an example of the meditative tendency of the Hebrew mind. The Greek mind delighted to consider events in their relations, one event as necessarily leading on another; and so a series of events, in which there was unity, formed, when that unity was exhibited, a drama. The Hebrew mind, on the other hand, is idyllic. It loves to pore over a thought, examining it from many points of view, stating and restating it, brooding upon it, seeing in it not so much a problem to be solved as a theme to be meditatively dwelt upon. The genius of its language is opposed to structural unity. It has no conception of a sentence formed otherwise than by addition; its only conjunction is "and." Of clauses main and subordinate, relative and causal, it knows nothing. It therefore rarely attempts to advance by steps to a conclusion. So the Book of Job, while we may call it dramatic because of its various stages and conclusion, yet has really no progress in it. It ends where it began, with the problem of the suffering of the righteous still unsolved, the voice of the Almighty silencing questions, but not answering them. So Jesus gave no systematized constitution of His kingdom, but He illustrated many aspects of it: "The kingdom of heaven is like . . ." In the centuries however between the Book of Job and the Apocalypse the influence of Greek thought had been affecting the Hebrew mind, and the form of the Apocalyptic drama is therefore far more Greek than Hebrew. But it shows its Oriental birth in its use of concrete symbols instead of abstract thoughts. The Western mind strips off from an idea all that is circumstantial and special and uses the abstract result as a term to think with. The Oriental mind will have nothing to do with abstractions, but must embody its thought in a concrete form. We are inclined, in trying to think in this way, to limit our thoughts either to the special image or to its significance. For the Oriental this breach does not exist, but the symbol and what it connotes are the same. This is why apocalyptic works, such as the books of Daniel and Enoch, abound in visions of horses and dragons and various beasts. It was not that the writer saw these very creatures, but that he translated his thought into these concrete terms, just as modern metaphysicians translate theirs into abstract terms, neither set expressing fully the conception of the writer, and the nomenclature in each case having to be learned before he can be understood. There may have been another reason also why the ideas of an apocalyptic writer should have been expressed not too plainly. Apocalypses always spring from a dissatisfaction with the state of things as they are, and the downfall of the existing government therefore has usually a prominent place in them. In the Apocalypse of St. John the fall of the Roman Empire is announced as near at hand. If it had been uttered too plainly, it would have attracted too much attention in official quarters. Apocalyptic literature must always speak chiefly to the initiated.

Ancient drama, unlike the modern, had no formal divisions into acts and scenes. Objection may therefore be raised to the imposition of this apparently modern form upon the Book of the Revelation; and exception may perhaps especially be taken to the dividing line here made between the fourth and fifth acts. But the particular points of division which may be adopted are of little importance. The main thing to be recognized is that the poem proceeds by four or five great steps, and that in developing each of these, subordinate ideas or *motifs* are introduced. Call these acts and scenes, or call them divisions and subdivisions, it matters little, so long as the skeleton of the work is felt as a sustaining power to its various members, and a guide to the understanding of their functions, individually and collectively.

It is interesting to note the difference of attitude toward the Roman Empire exhibited in the Apocalypse from that in St. Paul's Epistles. To St. Paul, proud of his Roman citizenship, the State was a friend, which the Christian should respect and obey. It saved him from a Jewish mob at Jerusalem (Acts xxi. 30–34), and its magic name delivered him from torture (Acts xxii. 25–30). It is to him God's vicegerent (Rom. xiii. 1; Tit. iii. 1), embodying His authority (Rom. xiii. 4). He never came in contact with the practice of

Dramatic Character of the Apocalypse 15

compelling the Christians as a test of their Christianity to burn incense to the statue of the Emperor, the personification of the State. This custom belongs to a succeeding reign. A change took place in the policy of the Empire toward the Christians. Before the year 64 A.D. a Christian was not put to death as such, but proof was required that he had been guilty of some act prejudicial to society. After this, however, it was assumed that all Christians were guilty of such hostility, and might be at once condemned on confession of the Name.[1] It was the latter policy which prevailed when the author of the Apocalypse wrote. He had seen the glare of burning Rome in the year 64, and the ghastly tortures of the Christians there and throughout the provinces. The martyrs of Smyrna, of Pergamos (ii. 10–13), and of the whole Christian world (vi. 9–12) stood before him, clamoring for vengeance on their oppressor, and making faithfulness to the cause seem

[1] Cf. "The Church in the Roman Empire," Prof. W. H. Ramsay, p. 243.

the one climactic virtue (ii. 7, et al.). His attitude therefore toward the State is that of determined hostility. The Church is now persecuted by the State (Ch. xii.); but her enemy — and what other name can the enemy have than that of the ancient arch-enemy, Babylon? — will be overthrown and destroyed (Ch. xviii.). He interrupts his narrative of the catastrophe with a burst of exultation over her downfall, which recalls the fierce denunciations of the Imprecatory Psalms: "Rejoice over her, thou heaven, and ye saints, apostles, and prophets, for God hath avenged you on her!" (xviii. 20).

The date of the Book of the Revelation is probably the latter half of the year 68 A.D. The author knew of the great fire at Rome in the year 64 (Ch. xviii.), and he shows apparently no acquaintance with the fall of Jerusalem, which took place in the year 70. Whether he was the Apostle John has been much discussed. The epithet "The Divine," in the title of the Book, is not in any early manuscript. This name was applied to the

Apostle John during the Arian controversy of the fourth century, in the belief that he was the author, by those who wished to emphasize the authority of the Book against the Arians. It is a name, not an adjective; meaning not "holy" but "theologian." Whoever the author was, he was probably a Jewish Christian, one, that is, who regarded Christianity as a reform of Judaism, not a successor to it. To us, with our eyes guided by history, it seems plain from the first that Judaism had been superseded by Christianity; but to the men of the apostolic age this was by no means evident. There were many of them who regarded Jesus as the Messiah, who saw no reason why they should not observe the Law and carry their sacrifices to the Temple as they had always done. It was Paul who first saw clearly that the dominance of the new meant the subsidence of the old; and it was largely on this account that he was distrusted and opposed, not only by Jews but by his fellow-Christians of Jewish descent. One of these latter was probably the author of the Apocalypse. He sees the Messiah's kingdom, its king, the inhabitants of it, and the punishment of its enemies, from a Jewish point of view. When the nations of the earth are saved, they are still regarded as over against the twelve tribes of Israel (vii. 9).[1] The wedding-garment of the Church is the righteousness of the saints (xix. 8), that is, the prescribed acts of obedience to the Law. The new Jerusalem has but twelve gates, and each of these bears the name of one of the tribes (xxi. 12). Jesus is for the author preëminently the Jewish Messiah, the Son of David (v. 5). St. Paul is either denounced throughout the Book or at least ignored. He has no place among the twelve apostles of the Lamb, which are the only basis of the Church of God (xxi. 14). The Church of Ephesus established by St. Paul is especially praised because it has "tried them which say they are apostles and are not, and hast found them liars" (ii. 2), words which cannot but recall the almost

---

[1] Cf. also "οἱ μικροί" (xix. 5).

identical language St. Paul himself uses of his opponents of the Jewish-Christian party (Gal. ii. 6, 9; 2 Cor. xii. 11). The doctrines of the Nicolaitanes and Balaamites (ii. 14, 15) are a distortion of those ascribed to St. Paul, and of the side which he took when the question of Gentile conformity was brought before the Church at Jerusalem (Acts xv. 29, cf. also 1 Cor. viii. and ix. 5). To the mind of the author throughout there is but one Church, the old Church of Judaism, which remains unshaken by recent heresies, and which is to develop a purified Jerusalem, where all who are saved of all nations are to find their home. Such is the theological position of the author in regard to party.

The setting, so to call it, of his vision comes very largely from the books of Ezekiel and Daniel. Daniel's mystic numbers with much of his Persian angelology and demonology reappear. Assyria, which for lack of quarries was compelled to import its stone, and which thus had slabs cut in relief rather than statues, probably showed to Ezekiel its human-headed winged bulls, such as are now preserved in our museums, and furnished him with the imaginative basis for his visions of wheels and cherubim (Ezek. i. and x.). Through him these impressed themselves upon later apocalyptic literature, and gave birth to the strange beasts that appear in the Book of the Revelation.

The author's mind is filled with the literature of his nation, and it is hard to tell whether its tone is more Jewish or Christian. The Book shows us, in fact, the union, so far as union is possible, of Judaism and Christianity. In the Old Testament we see Judaism. In St. Paul's Epistles we see the most distinctive features of Christianity. In the Gospels we see the two streams flowing side by side. But in the Revelation we see them mingled, with no consciousness on the part of the author that the result is not homogeneous.

The apocalypse was the ancient form of what we now call the philosophy of history. It aimed to classify events, to point out their laws and significance, to show their connection with the received scheme of the universe and their reach into the future, and to forecast that future in its necessary mould. And so the Apocalypse of St. John, dramatic as it is in form, stands as the great Epic of the Church, the first Philosophy of Christian History.

CHAPTER II

SIGNS OF THE TIMES

THE philosophy of history as a science may be claimed as a modern discovery, but the belief that history has a philosophy was even more common in ancient times than in modern, the belief that events were part of a plan and were a prelude to something greater than themselves. This, which might almost be said to constitute the Hebrew conception of history, would of course become more prominent in the popular mind at certain times; at those times when, as we say, a great crisis seems imminent. Such a crisis, foreseen by the prophets, was called in their language a "day of the Lord," and a frequent burden of their prophetic work was to announce that the "day" was at hand.

Such a time was the middle of the sixth century B.C., when the Jewish nation had been for thirty years in captivity at Babylon, the time which produced among other works the second half of the Book of Isaiah. Such a time was the reign of Antiochus Epiphanes, which gave birth to the Maccabean struggle and to the Book of Daniel. And such a time was this in the year 68 A.D., which produced the Apocalypse of St. John.

Together with the belief in the speedy coming of the Lord already mentioned was the belief that His advent was to be preceded by signs. Wars, civil commotions, wonders occurring in the sky and on the earth, pestilences and earthquakes, these were, according to the prophets (cf. Joel ii. 10, 30, 31 ; iii. 15 ; Isa. xiii. 9, 10), the precursors of the coming of the great Day of the Lord. And if ever the course of events seemed to justify a belief that the end of the world was at hand, certainly it was in the middle of the first century. In the year 64 occurred the great fire at Rome, which lasted for nine days.

Whatever may have been the belief of Nero or of the people in general as to the connection of the Christians with it, it was the occasion for a bloody massacre of them. Their Master had told them they should be as lights (λύχνοι) in the world. They became such literally, as many of them, clothed in shirts of pitch and bound each to a stake, were burned to satisfy the mob and light the Emperor home. This was the first of that series of persecutions which was to make the early centuries the heroic age of the Church. The Empire had long been showing signs of the inherent weakness of Nero's government, and in March 68 an unmistakable sign was given by the revolt of the army in Gaul under Vindex. This was followed in April by the revolt of Galba in Spain. The great Roman Empire, whose stability men had felt to be bound up with that of the world, seemed breaking up. In June the army at Rome joined the revolt and proclaimed Galba Emperor. Then the Senate declared Nero a public enemy and condemned him to death. When he saw that all was lost he escaped to the villa of Phaon, one of his freedmen, and here, after begging the few who still remained with him to kill him, he was at last stabbed in the throat by Epaphroditus, just in time to save him from being taken alive by the centurion despatched by the Senate. But exaggeration of value grew after death even in the case of Nero. He had always been popular with the crowd, who were fond of games, liked his buffoonery, and did not dislike his cruelty. And now men began to wish him back again. Then it began to be whispered that after all he was not dead; that the wound in his throat had been healed, and that at the instigation of the Parthian ambassador at Rome he had taken refuge in Parthia at the court of the Arsacidæ. It is not surprising that doubts of his death should have seemed reasonable. There had been only four persons present at the time, and the body had been cared for and buried privately by three of the women who were still devoted to him. To realize the death of one who is well known without having seen him dead, is difficult even for those who are intelligent and imaginative, while for those who are not imaginative and not intelligent such realization is almost impossible. So it is not strange that a firm belief sprang up that Nero was still alive in some quarter of the East, and that he would soon return at the head of an Eastern army to overthrow his enemies and unite opposing factions. And with this belief there was a party of his friends strong enough to set up again his statues and to issue edicts over his signature (cf. xiii. 11–18). For eighteen months no one of the generals of the legions in revolt could succeed in putting down his rivals and making good his own claim to priority. It was no wonder that the world trembled. For all the nations which made up the complex mass known as the Roman Empire, however much they might wish certain conditions of life under it to be different, were yet united in wishing it in the main to be preserved. All except Judæa; for the death of Nero, and the anarchy prevalent through the rest of the world, made a pause in the Roman preparations for the coming siege of Jerusalem, and gave the Jews hope of liberty once more. To them the fall of Rome would be indeed the beginning of the longed-for Messianic kingdom. It was no wonder, too, that with such a belief in the existence of Nero and his return, false Neros should appear here and there throughout the Empire, personating the Emperor, and that these should intensify in the public mind the conviction which had made their rise possible.

The materials out of which signs and wonders are made have existed in every age. The more intelligent the ages or the persons, and the more convinced that every event is not an independent happening, but is interwoven with a far-reaching chain, so much the more will they feel confident that each event has a significance beyond itself. It depends upon the amount of knowledge they happen to possess whether a red glow flashing along the sky signifies to them a datum for the discovery of a law of nature or the fall of an empire. All ages have signs, but different ages interpret them differently. And to the thoughtful mind of the middle of the first century the strange natural phenomena which had been taking place were signs that something mysterious was at hand. Brilliant meteors had been seen in the sky. The year 66 was the period of the earth's passage through that belt of aerolites which cuts our orbit every thirty years, and showers of shooting stars seemed to show that the very heavens could fall. Eclipses verified the words of the prophet, and men saw the sun turned into darkness and the moon into blood. The palpitating glow of the red and pale aurora seemed to open heaven and give men glimpses of the combat of the spiritual hosts of good and evil. Just off the coast of Asia in the Ægean Sea, ten miles from that Patmos which the author of the Apocalypse claimed as its birthplace, lay the volcanic island of Thera, the modern Pantorin, which for several years before the year 69 was in a period of eruption. Vesuvius was preparing for its great outbreak in the year 79; and already in February, 63, Pompeii had been almost ingulfed by an earthquake. If, as was undoubtedly the case, the author of the Apocalypse had been at Rome, it is not improbable that he would, like St. Paul, have disembarked at Puteoli, and have seen on his way to Rome Lake Avernus and that series of small volcanic craters, pits apparently bottomless, reeking with sulphur and vapor, the very ground sending up jets of smoke, craters which the ancients believed to be the mouths of the infernal regions, the abode of fallen Titans and evil spirits. Fifty years before, forty towns of Lydia had been destroyed by an earthquake at one blow. In the years 37, 46, 51, and 53 earthquakes were more or less extensively felt throughout Greece, Asia, and Italy. In 60 almost the whole valley of the Lycus was thus destroyed, and after 59 there was hardly a year which was not marked by some disaster of the kind. Wars, too, were going on in every quarter. The death of Nero had at once caused civil war among the Roman legions whose commanders were ambitious. Jerusalem had not yet fallen, but the Roman armies which had been sent to subjugate Judæa had perpetrated bloody massacres in Galilee. There was war beyond the Euphrates, among the Parthians. In addition to the fact that war then was in some respects more horrible in its circumstances and consequences than now, there was one of its incidental results which has now wholly disappeared. When a number of prisoners had been taken, the amphitheatres of the chief cities of the victorious countries were supplied with them for combat with the beasts and for the gladiatorial games, and foreign cities also supplied their amphitheatres by buying numbers of them. In days, too, before transportation had been made a science, the destruction of the crops and food of a country meant not only poverty for the people, but starvation. Famine's dark horse was a natural follower of the red horse of war; and on other occasions, too, it had appeared recently. In 68 the exportation of grain from Alexandria was insufficient for the market dependent on it. A sudden inundation of the sea had shortly before spread desolation throughout Lycia. In 65 a terrible pestilence broke out at Rome and carried off thirty thousand, and in the same year Campania had been ravaged by cyclones, whose destruction extended to the very walls of Rome. If we wish to trace the local color which fills the Apocalypse, and find the sources from which it rose to tinge the author's mind, we must remember that intelligence travelled more slowly then and portents made a deeper impression, and we must look not at Jerusalem only, not only at Ephesus and Rome, but through all the countries bordering the Mediterranean on its centre and east, and even as far as the Euphrates, which had not yet ceased to be the centre of the power of the Old World.

The twenty-fourth chapter of St. Matthew's Gospel in its present form dates probably from about this time. In it Jerusalem has apparently been compassed with armies, but has not yet fallen. But whatever may be its date, it represents the feeling of the Christian mind of the time, that before the coming of the Lord to set up His kingdom on earth—a consummation of all things which was to be expected speedily—there would be a general upheaval of the natural, political, and social worlds, and that when the whole universe seemed thus to be in travail, it was the sign that the Lord was at hand. And now in the years 68 and 69 the signs on every side seemed telling thoughtful believers with unmistakable plainness that the time was fulfilled and the Day of the Lord was but a few years off at the most. Our expectations of the manner in which the Kingdom of Heaven is to conquer the world are different from those of the Christians of the first century. We believe—those of us who believe at all—that the Kingdom is advancing gradually on every side, as the silent tide creeps slowly up a long reach of sand, and that it is little by little changing the nature of the world from within. But to the majority of the early Christians its method was rather that of a revolt which exists in secret, with its members known to one another and its plans matured, which has little or no present effect on society, but at the fixed time will suddenly break out and carry all before it, to the astonishment and dismay of those who are not enrolled among its members. Attention was consequently turned not so much to a gradual growth in righteousness, either for the world, or, in some cases, as we see from the Epistles to the Thessalonians, for themselves. What did it matter how they passed the few short days before all would be made new? Their gaze was wholly fixed on the future. Yet a little while, their Master had said while He was with them, and they should not see Him; but yet again a little while and they should see Him. And oh, the joy when they should look upon Him once more, coming through the clouds with thousands of His saints, and they who now were despised should find the day of their glory begun, and the world should see their trust justified!

It was this message of encouragement and consolation that the Book of the Revelation was designed to give. The Day of the Lord was surely at hand. The marvels which had been taking place in the physical and political worlds, while they filled the minds of other men with alarm, were to them, the Christians, the joyful signs that their deliverance was drawing nigh. And with the vision of their Lord standing and sending a message of warning and comfort to His Church, the poem opens.

CHAPTER III

THE DRAMA

THE proper action of the Apocalyptic drama unfolded for the consolation and strengthening of the waiting Church does not begin until Chapter four. What precedes consists of a Title, a Prologue, and a Salutation. After stating briefly the aim of the book in the Title (i. 1–4), the author draws out into a Prologue (i. 4–20) the *motifs* briefly mentioned in the Title — the purpose of the book, its authority, and the assurance of the near approach of the Lord's advent, with words of warning and comfort. To the Greek, inspiration came oftenest through the ear; to the Hebrew, through the eye. The old Greek poet invoked the Muse and listened carefully to hear her voice, whether within him or with-

Title
Prologue

out him. It was a δαίμων, an inward monitor which, Socrates said, gave him imperative direction. But the Hebrew prophet, as he sat meditating, saw before him visions, in which problem and answer revealed themselves clothed in concrete forms. And so, as the prophets prefaced the announcement of their visions with a "Thus saith the Lord," the author of the Revelation tells in the Prologue, in a way which must have reminded his readers of the calls of Isaiah (Isa. vi.) and Ezekiel (Ezek. i. and ii.), how he was commissioned by the Divine messenger whom he saw with the burden which he was about to deliver.

It was the Lord's Day, and he was "in the spirit," when suddenly he heard behind him a voice clear and sonorous as a trumpet. He turns to see the speaker, and there before him is the figure of his risen Lord; not now as when He stood before Pilate, nor as when He walked with His disciples in the fields of Galilee, but clothed with majesty and power. With the habit of mind already referred to, the Seer ascribes to the figure of his vision attributes which do not make a unity when literally interpreted by the understanding, but which are symbols for the imagination. The figure which he sees is like that of a man clothed in priestly dress, one who corresponds to the lofty type seen in former Apocalyptic visions (cf. Dan. x. 6), who yet bears also likeness to Almighty God (i. 8, 11). His hair is white with the wisdom of age, His eyes glow with the fire of youth, and His whole face is dazzling in its brilliance. His feet are firm and stable, His words are sharp and powerful, and His voice is like that of the sea. It is the risen Christ, the world's soon-appearing King. The Seer falls prostrate before Him in awe. But the Divine being raises him and gives him His commission, bidding him bear the message he shall receive to the Seven Churches of Asia. Jesus had said that a faithful disciple of His was like a candle fitted to its due candlestick. So here the Seven Churches appear surrounding their Master as well-appointed lamps, standing beside Him, as the great seven-branched candelabrum stood near the altar of incense in the Temple (2 Chron. xiii. 11).

Then comes the Salutation (Chs. ii. and iii.), the address to the audience, as it were, before the drama begins. The use of seven as a perfect number makes it probable that it was the Christian Church throughout Asia Minor that the author had in view as audience, and not only the seven particular churches specified; especially since we find here (i. 3) the same directions for having the missive read in the churches that St. Paul was accustomed to give (Col. iv. 16).

Salutation

The first Act then begins, which has to do with the Day of the Lord as made ready by the Roman Empire. First comes an introduction to the Act, descriptive of the scenery. The Seer looks through a window which is opened in the sky and sees Heaven. The same mighty being whose appearance had been described in the Prologue then transports him into the midst

Act I

of Heaven, and afterward accompanies him from place to place in it (xxii. 8), as Virgil served for guide to Dante. Here is the Court of Heaven, seen in the midst of its ordinary occupations, just as it is eternally while men are going about their daily pursuits. In the midst of Heaven he sees God sitting on His throne, surrounded by a rainbow. It is noteworthy how completely the best traditions of Hebrew religious usage, that God could not be visibly represented, and that His very name was unspeakable, had penetrated the national imagination and literature. His original name indeed, unpronounced for many centuries, had become lost; so that when men saw the letters which stood in part for it, they could only, with a mixture of reverence and ignorance, call it "the Lord." On this subject the literary imagination had no materials with which to work. The author of the Revelation could find in the prophets and the more recent Apocalyptic literature plenty of material from which to construct his visions of the Court of Heaven and of the Last Judgment, of Jesus as the King of glory, and of the new Jerusalem. But when it attempted to picture God, it was powerless. He could say nothing but "He that sat on the throne was to look upon like a jasper and a sardine stone." In that Divine aspect were blended something of the glow and passion of the ruby, something of the clearness and depth of the diamond. That was all he could say. The rainbow was a part of the furniture of the Divine throne, like the sceptre which to us is associated with the throne of an earthly king, and when it appeared in the sky it was regarded as lent for the occasion and therefore as a mark of special grace (cf. Gen. ix. 12–18). But here it stands in its normal place, while thunder and lightning and voices come perpetually from the throne. "In the midst of the throne," that is, in the semicircle before the throne, stand four composite Creatures, representative of the Divine attributes manifested in creation, and from them rises continually that voice of the universe in praise to God which the ear of the Hebrew poet was always hearing. These Creatures are another instance of the disregard of the Oriental mind in its symbolism for producing a unity for the understanding. It wishes to assert that its god is wise, and it ascribes to him the head of a man. It believes he is strong, and says he has the body of a bull. It aims to picture his omnipresence, and it represents him as having many wings or, as with the Indian gods, many arms. It wishes to ascribe to him the attributes of majesty and dominion, and it says that he is like a lion, or that seven thunders perpetually utter their voices in his presence. One detail after another is added to the image with no thought as to their material incongruity, nor their unnaturalness when pictured by the imagination. The demand that a poetic conception shall be naturalistically correct when imagined, is wholly a modern one, and when insisted on, often obscures from the spectator the author's conception. That the images described in the Apocalypse are unnatural and absurd when literally pictured, would not then have been felt as an objection, any more than we now feel it an objection to a statue that it has a color which no human being ever has.

Ranged in a semicircle, on each side of the throne, are seats for Twenty-four Elders, men of wisdom and age, representatives of worthy humanity, the Church; the number being taken from the twenty-four courses of the Jewish priesthood, or from the judicial council of the Sanhedrim.[1] These, from time to time, throughout the drama, together with the Four Creatures, act the part of the Greek chorus; never criticising, however, as that chorus did, but amplifying the *motif* which is being set forth and praising God. From the throne as a centre there stretches away on every side a vast expanse, like the sea, clear and shining. It is the floor of Heaven, the upper side of the sky, of that

[1] Dr. E. C. Selwyn ("The Christian Prophets and the Prophetic Apocalypse") thinks that the author's familiarity with judicial procedure indicates that he had been a member of the Sanhedrim.

"firmament" which the mind of antiquity conceived as forming the ceiling of the world. In the right hand of God is the Book of Fate, closed and sealed with seven seals; and when a celestial herald has proclaimed throughout Heaven a challenge to any one who is worthy, to come forward and open the seals, no one appears. Then when the Seer beholds this, when he sees the knowledge of the future, the only hope of the Christian, withheld from him, he bursts into tears. What is the use of beholding the secrets of Heaven if its most precious secret still remains hidden? But — and with this chapter the second scene of the Act begins — he is bidden not to weep, for one is found who is worthy to open the Book. And with this Jesus comes forward and takes the Book from the hand of God. As He takes it, a mighty chorus bursts forth from Heaven and earth and sky and sea, a chorus of praise to Him who has redeemed men, and who is about to reveal to them their future glory. The Four Creatures and the Twenty-four Elders fall down before Him; angels, whose ranks stretch off as far as the eye can reach, in number "ten thousand times ten thousand and thousands of thousands," take up the song; the earth from below, with all its living beings, is heard joining in the solemn chorus, which closes with a deep "Amen" from the Four Creatures who commenced it, while the Twenty-four Elders worship Him who holds the Book. Then Jesus the Christ begins to unfold it, opening one seal at a time. As each of the first four seals is opened, there comes a voice from one of the Four Creatures, like the pedal of an organ, "Come and see!"[1] while there passes across the stage a ghastly and grim procession. On their horses, white, red, black, and gray, appear, one after another, the victorious Roman Empire, with War, Famine, and Death. But as this terrible train passes on, and the fifth seal is opened, the attention of the Seer is directed to the altar which stands in the open space before the throne of God

[1] The Revisers' text omits the words " and see."

and the seats of the Elders, and to the cavity within it, corresponding to that into which, in the altar of the Jewish temple, the drink-offerings were poured. There he sees the souls of the martyrs — for the year 64 was still fresh in the memory of the Christian Church. They raise their voices to God, crying out for justice, and for the avenging of their blood on this terrible Roman Empire with its train. But no, the time is not yet come. The victor's white robe is given to each of them, and they are bidden to wait in patience for a while, until their brethren, who are yet to suffer as martyrs on the earth, shall join them. The sixth seal is opened, and the Seer beholds the convulsions of Nature, which had been filling men's minds, exhibited as indeed the precursive signs of the Day of the Lord, which now with the opening of the last seal may be expected to begin. The angels who hold in check the four winds of the four quarters of the earth take their stations ready to loose the winds for the earth's final destruction. But an angelic herald comes hurrying from Heaven, bidding them delay until the righteous have been preserved from the evil that is coming, that they may not be overtaken by the catastrophe which is to overwhelm the wicked. Then, as the Israelites in Egypt were marked that the destroyer might pass over them, he proceeds to seal the elect in their foreheads, with God's signet, which he carries; and the Seer, from his post in Heaven, hears announced the number of those who are sealed. It is 144,000, the complete number of all the tribes of Israel. At the same moment this great host becomes visible, standing before God's throne, clothed, like the victors in the games, with white robes, and palm branches in their hands. As they raise a chorus of thanksgiving to God for their deliverance, all the angels and Elders and the Four Creatures break out again into the song which they sang before, ending with the same deep "Amen." And while the Seer stands gazing at this great multitude, one of the Elders tells him who they are. "These are they which came out of great tribulation, and have washed their robes and made them white in the blood of the Lamb. Therefore, are they before the throne of God and serve Him day and night in His temple; and He that sitteth on the throne shall dwell among them. They shall hunger no more, neither thirst any more; neither shall the sun strike on them, nor any heat. For the Lamb which is in the midst of the throne shall feed them, and shall lead them unto living fountains of waters; and God shall wipe away all tears from their eyes."

The seventh seal is opened. And now we expect the fulfilment of all things and the end of time. But, as says a writer who has ably set forth the dramatic nature of the Apocalypse,[1] "the fundamental idea of the poem is to show the Great Judgment continually postponed at the moment when it seems as if it must take place.[2] . . . In the

[1] Renan, "L'Antechrist," Ch. xvi. pp. 388, 391.

[2] For a similar suspension of the dramatic development, cf. that which takes place after the opening of the fifth and sixth seals; also x. 6, *l.c.*

poem, as in reality, the catastrophe is forever fleeing. Now, we think, it has arrived; but nothing occurs. In place of the final *dénoûment*, which was to be the result of the opening of the seventh seal, there is a silence in Heaven for half an hour, indicating that the first Act of the Mystery is ended and another is about to begin."[1]

The first Act was the opening of the seals, and pointed chiefly to the Roman Empire and its train as precursive signs of the coming of the Day of the Lord. The second Act is the sounding of the archangels' trumpets, and deals chiefly with the convulsions of nature, which had been taking place. These the author has indeed referred to (vi. 12), but he now dwells on them more in detail. But as the seven archangels, whose place is before God's throne, are about to blow the trumpets which are now given them, there occurs an episode or introductory scene, as in the

Act II

[1] The division into chapters and verses in the A. V. is of course to be disregarded; viii. 1 is properly the conclusion of Ch. vii, just as xxii. 2, *f.c.*, belongs to xxii. 1, as in the R. V.

case of the first, third, and fourth Acts.[1] An angel comes to the altar, which stands in the semicircle before the Elders' seats and the throne, and throws incense upon it; and as the smoke rises, he fills his censer with the coals and casts them down to the earth. The incense, we are told, is the prayers of the saints; and these prayers, rising in silence to God, and calling for the destruction of the wicked world where the saints have suffered, turn to burning coals, destroying and consuming the earth wherever they strike.

And now the seven archangels prepare to sound the trumpets which they hold. At the sound of the first trumpet there bursts upon the earth a storm with lightning and bloody hail. At the sound of the second a volcanic island appears in the sea (cf. what was said of Thera, p. 24). At the sound of the third a burning meteor falls from Heaven. With the fourth a darkness as of an eclipse —a phenomenon always mysterious and ter-

[1] Cf. Chs. iv., xi., xv.

rible in early ages — covers the earth. As the fifth angel sounds, the entrance to the infernal regions is unclosed, and with the smoke that streams forth there comes an army apparently of scorpions which spread over the earth and work destruction upon it; but as this is a Divine plague, it is commanded not to harm God's sealed elect. Possibly the imagination of the Seer had for its basis in this vision the sulphurous pits filled with noxious reptiles near Puteoli, to which reference has already been made.[1]

After the sounding of the fourth trumpet there occurs some delay — a delay which recurs after the fifth and sixth trumpets also. It is, as has been said,[2] a part of the plan of the poem to exhibit the delays in the establishment of Christ's Kingdom, under which it was so hard to remain faithful, as part of God's eternal purpose, and therefore as steps, not hindrances, to the Kingdom's development. The non-appearance of the Kingdom must therefore be not disregarded, but emphasized.

[1] p. 29.   [2] p. 47.

The first five trumpets have been followed by convulsions of nature. The sixth brings with it a plague which must have seemed as startling as any convulsion of nature, so sudden and destructive and terrible was it whenever it occurred. In the absence of the means of rapid communication, the coming of an invading army was often not announced until it fell upon the destined country, and all the convulsions of nature combined could hardly be more disastrous than such an army's presence. The whole Roman world had for a long time been expecting almost daily an invasion of the Parthians. And now the Seer beholds the dreaded Parthian cavalry pouring forth from beyond the Euphrates, breathing out fire and smoke and destroying a third of mankind. But all these plagues have no regenerating effect upon the world. Men still continue in their evil ways, and by so doing make more imminent the judgment of the Day of the Lord, which is to burst upon the earth at the sounding of the seventh trumpet. All things are prepared for the end. A herald comes from God, and standing with one foot on the sea and the other on the land utters in a mighty voice the secrets of the future. The Seer is about to write and announce the mystery of the Kingdom of Heaven thus revealed to him, when he is bidden to desist. The secrets of God can never be told in a word nor learned in a moment. Experience alone can reveal them to men. And so here again as in the first Act, the end of all things, ever imminent, is ever postponed. Instead of the sound of the last trump there comes a delay. The mighty herald promises that there shall soon be delay (A. V. "time") no longer, but that when the seventh angel's trumpet shall sound the mystery of God shall be finished. Meanwhile the Seer is told that his burden is not simply to announce the deep things of God, — how easy if that were the preacher's only work! — but that he has a mission in translating generals into particulars; he must reveal their destinies to many rulers and nations. And thus, his imagination filled with the striking figure of the old prophet (Ezek. iii. 1), who represented himself as devouring the written words of God, the Seer takes from the angelic herald the Book containing the destinies of the nations and eats it. After he has eaten it, he is at once filled with a new message, and with the mingling of sweetness and pain which it is the characteristic of divine truth, when vividly felt, to inspire.

Here is the turning-point in the action of the drama. Hitherto the first and second Acts have had reference chiefly to events which had actually taken place on the earth, or were taking place at the time the author wrote, his aim being to show them as signs of the coming of the Day of the Lord. But now he passes to the future. He sees the Kingdom of Heaven established, as indeed it will be in a short time; and the remainder of his poem is occupied with portraying the results for the saints and for the wicked nations of the world, of its establishment.

Jerusalem must inevitably be the scene of action; for the Jewish imagination, even when joined with Christian ideas, could conceive of no other place as the radiating centre of the Kingdom of Heaven upon earth. The Seer now has revealed to him the events which are to take place in the short time, three years and a half, which is to elapse before the kingdom is established at Jerusalem. The three years and a half, forty-two months, must be taken as a round number, though the writer sometimes computes it in days for the sake of greater apparent certainty. It is just half of the sacred week of seven years which played so prominent a part in the Jewish social economy (cf. Lev. xxv. 1–7), and which is sometimes used, like the numbers 3 , 7, 12, and 40 in other connections, to express unity of time. It was the current belief in the Jewish Church that a divine witness would be sent, before the advent of the

Messiah, to announce His coming and prepare the world for it (cf. Mal. iv. 5, 6; St. John i. 19, 25; St. Matt. xvi. 14). It was also a widespread belief that the final judgment would be preceded by two witnesses, who would "pacify the wrath of the Lord's judgment before it broke forth into fury, and turn the heart of the father unto the son, and restore the tribes of Jacob" (Ecclus. xlviii. 10). These messengers were differently identified with Enoch, Moses, Elijah, and Jeremiah.[1] In the passage now before us the author may have had in view two persons of prominence in the Church, then or recently living in Jerusalem. At all events, the two prophetic witnesses whose life and words are to usher in the great judgment are seen undergoing in these three years and a half the fate of all outspoken witnesses to the truth: prophesying, accomplishing wonders, bearing down opposition, but finally overcome and killed, amid the exultation of those who felt their

[1] Cf. with this belief, St. Matt. xvii. 3.

presence a rebuke to themselves. But these two martyrs do not have to wait for their justification, for they are at once raised from the dead and taken up into Heaven, while a great earthquake shakes the world. Their exulting enemies, alarmed by this apotheosis and the earthquake, are converted and give glory to God.

The fulness of the Gentiles is now come in, and there is no more occasion for delay. The seventh angel sounds. It is the last trump so long expected which is to bring in the Kingdom of the glory of the Lord and of His Christ. At once solemn voices proclaim throughout Heaven that the Kingdom is established. The Twenty-four Elders fall down before God and worship with their choral song: —

"We give Thee thanks, Lord God Almighty, which art and which wast, because Thou hast taken Thy great power and dost reign. And the nations were wroth, and Thy wrath is come, and the time of the dead is come to be judged, and the time to give their reward to Thy servants the prophets, and to the saints, and to them that fear Thy name, the small and the great, and to destroy them that destroy the earth."

The Kingdom of God is established. The great event for which the Christian heart has waited with longing has happened. But the mind of the Seer has been so long occupied with signs that he cannot turn at once from this employment, so congenial to Apocalyptists, to seize and set forth merely the central facts of the glory of the newly established Kingdom with its results affecting the good and the evil on the earth. The logical development of a plan is not to be expected of him. He is less concerned with due proportion in the unfolding of his plot than with pouring forth the visions with which his imagination has been filled by the older Apocalypses. In the third Act, in the twelfth and thirteenth chapters, he gives a series of visions which have comparatively little to do with the movement of the drama, though they enrich

Act III

it with color, and were no doubt adapted to the consolation of those who lived in the midst of the events they symbolically describe.

The first of these visions is of the Church, that is, the Jewish Church. To us who see the long centuries of the life of Christianity and its clearly developed individual existence, it is difficult to conceive it as a mere phase, even an improved phase, of Judaism. But to the devout Jewish Christian of the first century, the Church of his fathers, stretching back indefinitely into the past, was still the only Church, and Christianity, with all its wonderful future, to him unforeseen, was but a passing phase of it. In his vision the Seer looks back and sees the Church in travail with her mysterious birth, the Messiah. He sees the persecutions to which she is subjected by her arch-enemy, the Roman Empire, with its seven Cæsars and ten provincial proconsuls. And he sees that the contest between the woman and the dragon is but a part of the mighty war going on in Heaven, as well as on earth, between the powers of good and of evil.

Strict consistency in the use of images and their mutual exclusiveness must no more be demanded from an Apocalyptist than fidelity to nature. That he has represented an idea in one form is no bar to his representing it in another. And so in his next vision the Roman Empire, just now a dragon, becomes a beast from across the sea, having the same chief marks as before, seven heads and ten horns; but this time attention is drawn to one of the heads, which has in it a deadly wound, partly or wholly healed. The dragon of the previous vision, even in it, was alternately the Roman Empire and Satan — for were not the two synonymous? And now Satan appears as this beast, while another beast, whose identification is doubtful, acts as assistant to the first and procurer of honor for him. The head with its deadly wound healed is so prominent in the writer's imagination that he speaks of it and of the beast to which it belongs as identical. He then gives the name of the beast in a form in which it would be known only to the initiated. "Here is wisdom," he exclaims; "let him that hath understanding count the number of the beast, for it is the number of a man; and his number is six hundred threescore and six."

Writing in cipher was as well known to the ancient world as to the modern; and the use of numbers for names, even where no other concealment is used, has often been a favorite form of cipher.[1] Sometimes the number is a purely arbitrary one. Sometimes, as here, its composition can be traced in the circumstances of the case. In most ancient languages each letter was also a numeral. The letters of a name then could be translated into figures, and these figures added into a number that should stand for the name it was desired to express covertly.

---

[1] "I was as confident, till you tell me you believe it, that the devil himself cannot decypher a letter that is well written, or find that 100 stands for Sir H. Vane." — *Correspondence of Edward Hyde, afterward Earl of Clarendon, with Dr. John Barwick, Feb.* 20, 1659–60.

The Drama

The letters of the name "Nero Cæsar" in its Hebrew form make up the number 666.[1] That care was necessary in connecting political personages or events with prophecy may be seen in a book some twenty years earlier in date, the Second Epistle to the Thessalonians, where the periphrases of St. Paul are almost as difficult to unravel as a cipher. He warns those to whom he writes that the Day of the Lord will not come "except the falling away come first, and the man of sin be revealed, the son of perdition, he that opposeth and exalteth himself against all that is called God or that is worshipped; so that he sitteth in the temple of God, setting himself forth as God. Remember ye not that when I was yet with you I told you these things? And now ye know what restraineth, to the end that he may be revealed in his own season. For the mystery of lawlessness

---

[1] נ = 50, ר = 200, ו = 6, ן = 50, ק = 100, ס = 60, ר = 200 = נרון קסר = 666.

The shorter Latin form for Nero, נרו, would give 616 which is mentioned by Irenæus as an ancient reading here for 666. For list of various opinions, cf. De Wette or Düsterdieck *in loc.*

doth already work; only there is one that restraineth now, until he be taken out of the way. And then shall be revealed the lawless one, whom the Lord Jesus shall slay with the breath of His mouth, and bring to nought by the manifestation of His coming, even he whose coming is according to the working of Satan, with all power and signs and lying wonders."[1] Such obscurity, obscure in the original as in the translation, could not have been accidental, but must have been intentional. It was designed to conceal the thought as well as to reveal it. St. Paul was saying in effect to his friends in Thessalonica: "He that hath ears to hear, let him hear. Unto you it is given to know the mysteries of the Kingdom of Heaven, but unto them that are without it is not given; that seeing, they may see and may not perceive, and hearing, they may not understand."[2]

[1] 2 Thess. ii. 3–10.

[2] Instances of cryptograms in the Old Testament are Jer. xxv. 26 ; where by using the second and twelfth letters from the end of the alphabet instead of from the beginning, "Sheshach" is written instead of "Babel," *i.e.* Babylon.

The Drama

So the author of the Revelation aimed to write in such a manner as should be intelligible to the initiated, but should pass unnoticed by the authorities or remain hidden from them. He has said it. The Beast, the arch-enemy of the Christian Church, the great Antichrist, is Nero, the mighty Emperor. Nero was still alive, according to the popular belief,[1] and would return from the East. And it will not seem surprising that the author, after having designated Nero by one of the heads of the Beast, should then think of the whole Beast as Nero, if we remember that the logic of a vision is spiritual rather than formal, and that its progress is not so much a necessary sequence of mutually exclusive ideas as a succession of pictures, which must seem arbitrary unless their inner connection is perceived.

But while the Seer's gaze is bent upon Jerusalem in these dark days of the last times, he sees a brighter vision. It is inter-

---

Also probably Isa. vii. 6, where by a different system " Tabeal " stands for " Remaliah."   [1] Cf. p. 25.

esting to note in the Old Testament the Jew's conviction that the moral worth of his nation's little strip of territory made it the peer of the broadest and most favored country in the word. Princes were to come out of Egypt, and Ethiopia was to stretch out her hands toward Israel on account of the God who dwelt within her borders.[1] So, too, Mount Zion, a hill in the southwestern part of Jerusalem, only 450 feet above the bottom of the valley at its base, was to the exultant mind of the Jew loftier than the highest of mountains. " The hill of God is as the hill of Bashan (*i.e.* Mount Hermon, the highest mountain known to the Hebrews), an high hill, as the hill of Bashan. Why leap ye, ye high hills? This is the hill which God desireth to dwell in!"[2] And now as the Seer's gaze is directed upon Jerusalem, he sees this spot, the centre of the world's righteousness, at last publicly exhibited as such. The Church, the true Israel, the 144,000 that comprise all the faith-

[1] Ps. lxviii. 31. [2] Ps. lxviii. 15, 16.

ful of the earth, appear surrounding their King upon the Temple-hill, Mount Zion. They break out into their choral song, which the listening Seer has already heard in Heaven, while the great orchestra of the universe, harps and thunders and "the voice of many waters," gives its accompaniment.

It lends perhaps color to the traditional belief that the Revelation was written at Patmos, to note how the author is impressed by the "voice of many waters" as one of the prominent and majestic tones of nature. No inland-dweller could have felt this; but there is a peculiar fitness in its selection as one of the elements of the heavenly orchestra, if we may think of it as perpetually sounding in the ears of the writer as he walked the rocky shores of Patmos. It is possible, too, that we may see a reflection of his insular condition in his statement that in the new Heaven and new earth which he saw "there was no more sea." His isolated position, if such it was, would have accentuated his race characteristics. For while to us the sea is a means of communication and civilization, to the Hebrews it was a type of separation and destructiveness and an object of dread. Greece, with its deeply indented coast, produced a nation of mariners and bound itself through them to every part of the world. The Hebrews, on the other hand, possessed but one port,[1] and their maritime commerce was always small. The sea held with them much the same place that the forest holds in mediæval literature,— a region lying beyond civilized habitations, largely unknown, and inhabited by strange beasts and strange men, into which prudent people did not venture. They knew but little about it from experience. As the Psalmist stood on a hill and looked upon the blue line of the Mediterranean in the distance, he saw more with his imagination than with his eyes: "This great and wide sea, wherein are things creeping innumerable,

[1] *I.e.* Joppa. Dor (cf. LXX.), Accho, Achzib, and Zidon were within the territory assigned to the tribe of Asher; but the Asherites never acquired possession of them. Cf. Judges i. 31, 32.

both small and great beasts. There go the ships. There is that leviathan, whom Thou hast formed to sport with him."[1] Those who go down to the sea have a special opportunity for seeing the dread works of the Lord in mighty waves, sea-sickness, storm, and calm.[2] The ships of Tarshish are enumerated among the worldly pomps which shall be brought low;[3] and though the ideal Jerusalem of the future shall be surrounded by broad rivers and streams, yet there shall be no boat nor ship upon them.[4] It was apparently not only a disapproval of the foreign policy of King Jehoshaphat, but also a feeling that naval affairs were unbecoming a godly man, which made the Chronicler take a grim satisfaction in recording that the king's ships, which he had taken such pains to construct, never made a voyage, for "they were broken, that they were not able to go to Tarshish."[5] And

[1] Ps. civ. 25, 26.
[2] Ps. cvi. 23–31.
[3] Isa. ii. 16.
[4] Isa. xxxiii. 21.
[5] 2 Chron. xx. 35–37.

to a non-seafaring people the threat for disobedience was peculiarly severe — that they should be carried back to Egypt "in ships."[1] But the conditions of the heavenly Kingdom precluded all alien, divisive elements, and therefore in the new earth there would be "no more sea."[2]

Now that the Kingdom of Jesus is thus set up on earth, three angels fly to the zenith and proclaim there, as from a new Sinai, the Law of the new Kingdom — that is, the everlasting Gospel — and announce the fall of the arch-enemy, Rome. The mention of Rome and of the Beast could but recall to every mind the persecutions of the year 64, in which so many of the faithful had perished, and also arouse again a question which troubled deeply the minds of the devout Christians of the middle of the first century. As they saw the years passing on, and one and another of their friends falling asleep,

---

[1] Deut. xxviii. 68.

[2] On the effect of the scenery of Patmos upon the author of the Revelation, cf. Dean Stanley's Sermons in the East, "Patmos."

while their Lord still delayed His coming, they anxiously asked what would be the condition of those who were not alive to see the Lord and to meet Him? Were they to be cut off from the blessed privileges of the Parousia? This is the matter which St. Paul explains so fully in several of his epistles.[1] And now the prophet of the Apocalypse hears a voice bidding him write for the comfort of such troubled souls that from this time henceforth those who die in the Lord are blessed as well as those who remain and are alive at His coming. "Blessed are the dead which die in the Lord," says the voice, "from henceforth." Then follow angels who represent symbolically the harvesting of the earth, the gathering-in of those on whom the judgment is to be passed.

Now begins a new Act of the drama. The faithful who have not done homage to the Beast are gathered out of the earth, so that the seven last

Act IV

---

[1] 1 Cor. xv. 50-53; 1 Thess. iv. 13-18; 2 Thess. i. 7-ii. 9.

plagues, which are to be sent upon the earth as its punishment, may not hurt them. Across the stage there passes a majestic procession. Out of the Temple come seven angels, clothed in white with girdles of gold, and as they pass the Four Creatures, one of the latter gives to each of them a golden bowl or vial, like that in which the priests offered the propitiatory blood in the Temple sacrifices, but this was "full of the wrath of God." When all have received the golden bowls, a voice comes from the Temple, "Go your ways, and pour out the vials of the wrath of God upon the earth." One after another the angels pass on and empty the bowls, and groan after groan arises, as plagues like those of Egypt — disease, blood, fire, and darkness — fall upon the earth and its inhabitants. According to popular belief, as already mentioned,[1] Nero was still alive beyond the Euphrates, and would return at the head of a Parthian army to regain his Empire. This appears, to the

[1] p. 25.

author of the Apocalypse,[1] an infernal plan, arranged by Satan, Nero, and his attendant.[2] For although the great battle which would follow the return of Nero would be in the first instance against the power of Rome, yet the author looks beyond this, regarding that return rather as the reëstablishment of the power of Antichrist, and the mighty battle which he foresees as the meeting of the powers of the world with spiritual powers. He beholds the armies of the kings of the earth gathered on the great battle-field of Hebrew history, — Armageddon, he calls it, — that little strip of land on which more battles have been fought than on any equal area in the world, the Plain of Esdraelon or Megiddo.[3] It lay just in the road between the empires of the north and east and that of Egypt, and across it the armies of centuries have marched and countermarched. It was the scene of the dramatic defeat of the Syrians under Sisera by the Hebrews under

[1] xvi. 12–15.   [2] xiii. 11.

[3] הַר מְגִדּוֹן, Har-Megiddon, the Hill of Megiddo.

Deborah, Barak, and Jael.[1] It was here that, a little later, occurred that great slaughter of the Midianites by Gideon's band,[2] which impressed itself on following ages as the type of a glorious victory for the Lord.[3] Here the young king Josiah, the one bright gleam in the falling fortunes of the Davidic dynasty, was slain,[4] a disaster which to the far-sighted seemed overwhelming.[5] Such, in fact, it proved. And on this spot where the house of David had received the blow which was its overthrow, here, the Seer foresaw, the Son of David would meet and conquer the kings of the nations and restore again the old Davidic kingdom in its true, spiritual form.

As the poem goes on, the mind of the writer becomes more and more filled with the judgment of the great enemy of the Church, Rome. As he has spoken of Nero by a cryptographic name, the number 666, and of Jerusalem as "Sodom" and "Egypt,"[6]

---

[1] Judges iv. [2] Judges vii. 8.
[3] Ps. lxxxiii. 11, 12. [4] 2 Chron. xxxv. 20–25.
[5] 2 Chron. xxxv. 25; Lam. iv. 20. [6] xi. 8.

so his mystical tendencies, as well as the exigencies of the case, lead him to employ a circumlocution in speaking of Rome. To him she is the ancient enemy of the Hebrew kingdom, Babylon; and as he paints the picture, rich in color and full of imaginative touches, of her destruction, his mind is filled with the images with which the old Hebrew prophets painted the destruction of Babylon and of Tyre.[1] If we may allow weight to slight indications of internal evidence, we may perhaps infer from the mention of Megiddo as the most natural battle-field, that the author was a Palestinian Jew who had often wandered over this plain; and again, from this intense bitterness against Rome, that he had been one of those faithful in the imperial city who had been intended for the martyrdom of the arena or the shirt of pitch in the Neronian persecution, but who had escaped the fate which overtook so many of his companions.[2] It is a fine picture that he

[1] Isa. xiii; Ezek. xxvi. 27.
[2] Cf. the tradition mentioned by Tertullian of St. John having escaped martyrdom in a caldron of boiling oil at Rome.

draws,— the woman, Babylon, "arrayed in purple and scarlet colour, and decked with gold and precious stones and pearls, having a golden cup in her hand," sitting on her seven hills; the city seen at a distance burning; while around there stand three groups watching. A group of the kings of the earth, "standing afar off for the fear of her torment," bewail her and lament for her. Another group of "shipmasters and sailors and as many as trade by sea," wail and cast dust upon their heads. A third group of the merchants of the earth weep for her and mourn that no man will buy their merchandise any more, "the merchandise of gold and silver and precious stones, and of pearls and fine linen and purple and silk and scarlet, and all thyine wood, and all manner vessels of ivory, and all manner vessels of most precious wood, and of brass and iron and marble and cinnamon and odours and ointments and frankincense and wine and oil and fine flour and wheat and beasts and sheep and horses and chariots and slaves and souls of men."[1]

[1] xviii. 12, 13.

As the prophet sees all this he exclaims in a tone of sternly exultant joy, "Rejoice over her, thou Heaven, and ye saints, apostles, and prophets, for God hath avenged you on her!" And the conclusion of the judgment of Babylon is uttered in a strain whose recurrent burden accentuates with its deep notes the hopelessness and finality of the doom: "And the voice of harpers and minstrels and flute-players and trumpeters shall be heard no more at all in thee;[1] and no craftsman, of whatsoever craft, shall be found any more at all in thee; and the sound of a mill-stone shall be heard no more at all in thee; and the light of a lamp shall shine no more at all in thee; and the voice of the bridegroom and of the bride shall be heard no more at all in thee; for thy merchants were the princes of the earth; for by thy sorceries were all nations deceived."[2] Then, as has so often in the course of the poem been the case, the scene shifts from earth to Heaven; the spiritual events

[1] Nero's posing as a connoisseur in music no doubt gave rise to a host of imitators at court and among the fashionable in society.   [2] xviii. 22, 23.

which are taking place are seen to be the same in both. The clouds roll asunder, and the Seer beholds the mighty heavenly chorus taking up the theme which has just been set forth on earth. The song begins and ends with the same deep chord, rising from the voices of the thousands that stretch off in ranks from the centre of Heaven. "'Alleluiah!'" they sing. "'Salvation and glory and honour and power unto the Lord our God! for true and righteous are His judgments. For He hath judged the great harlot which did corrupt the earth with her fornication, and hath avenged the blood of His servants at her hand.' And again they said, 'Alleluiah!' And her smoke rose up for ever and ever. And the Four and Twenty Elders and the Four Creatures fell down and worshipped God that sat on the throne, saying, 'Amen! Alleluiah!'"

Now comes the last Act of the Drama, the marriage of the Prince of Heaven, the final punishment of His enemies, and His assumption of His glory.

Act V

Heaven opens, and there appears a white horse and rider, armed for war. This is the Prince, who rides forth to His last short battle. His eyes glitter like fire; His garments are sprinkled with blood; on His head are many crowns; and on His dress and His girdle is emblazoned His heraldic device — "King of kings, and Lord of lords." All the armies of Heaven follow Him upon white horses, while, on the other hand, the Beast and the kings of the earth collect all their forces to meet them. But the combat is short. The Beast and his lieutenant, the False Prophet, are quickly taken, and their armies are totally destroyed. We are inclined to expect a fuller description of this battle than is given. But the writer's lack of art and form, and his interest in the wholly spiritual sides of his drama, impel him to hurry on to its conclusion.

Then appears the author's scheme of eschatology. The Devil is seized, and, not destroyed, but bound and cast into a bottomless pit, which is sealed for a thousand years.[1] But first comes a resurrection; not of all the dead, not of all the righteous dead, but of those only who had suffered martyrdom, or who had abstained from the worship of the Beast. These constitute a sort of aristocracy of the Kingdom of Heaven, and rise from their graves and reign on earth with Christ during the thousand years. The mind of the Seer was cast in the mould of the social system of his day, and if there was a king and a kingdom, the King must of course gather His nobles about Him. But it is to be noted that the basis of aristocracy is not birth nor official position, but purity and worth of character. The rest of the dead are not extinct; they wait until the millennium is ended. At the end of the thousand years the Devil is released from the bottomless pit, as if to ascertain whether his nature had been changed by his punishment, and to give even him one more chance. But he

[1] The duration of the period is apparently computed from poetic expressions which lead to the conclusion that "the Day of the Lord is as a thousand years." Cf. Ps. xc. 4; lxxxiv. 10; 2 Pet. iii. 8, 10.

immediately sets out upon his characteristic work of evil throughout the world. He collects a multitudinous army and besieges the saints in Jerusalem. But as the angel of the Lord had suddenly smitten an army besieging Jerusalem in ancient times,[1] so now the fire of God falls and consumes this army, while the Devil is cast into a lake of fire and brimstone. Then comes the general resurrection and the Last Judgment.

"And I saw a great white throne and Him that sat on it, from whose face the earth and the heaven fled away, and there was found no place for them. And I saw the dead, small and great, stand before God; and the books were opened, and another book was opened, which is the Book of Life, and the dead were judged out of those things which were written in the books, according to their works. And the sea gave up the dead which were in it, and death and the grave delivered up the dead which were in them,

---

[1] 2 Kings xix. 35.

and they were judged, every man according to his works."[1]

The last scene of the drama is the renewal of all things, a renewal so complete that Heaven itself shares in it, and the prophet sees "a new Heaven," as well as a new earth. The new earth is, however, conceived on the same plan as the old. Jerusalem is the centre of it, seen now in all her glory as the bride of God. On each of its glittering foundations — " The first foundation was jasper; the second, sapphire; the third, a chalcedony; the fourth, an emerald; the fifth, sardonyx; the sixth, sardius; the seventh, chrysolyte; the eighth, beryl; the ninth, a topaz; the tenth, a chrysoprasus; the eleventh, a jacinth; the twelfth, an amethyst" — on each glows the name of one of the twelve apostles; while every one who enters the Holy City must come in by one of its twelve gates; that is, must come as a member of one of the tribes of Israel. The mind of the Seer, poetic and creative as it is, does

[1] xx. 11, 14.

Ezekiel's idea of the restored community all the area surrounding the temple, and not merely one small spot within it, had become holy.[1] In Jeremiah's prophetic outlook the holy character extends to the city and its suburbs.[2] And when we turn to the Seer of the New Testament, we find that it is a city only which fills his vision. In the new Heaven and new earth all else has become absorbed in a city filled with multitudinous life; there is nothing but this. God is now limited to no one abode in it, since He permeates its every part. His dwelling-place is henceforth in no curtained tent, aloof from the Congregation, in no temple built with hands. It is in humanity itself.[3]

"And I heard a great voice out of heaven, saying, 'Behold the tabernacle of God is with men, and He will dwell among them, and they shall be His people, and God Himself shall be with them and be their God. And God shall wipe away all tears

[1] Ezek. xliii. 12.   [2] Jer. xxxi. 38 f.
[3] Rev. xxi. 3, 22, 23.

from their eyes, and there shall be no more death, neither sorrow, nor crying, neither shall there be any more pain; for the former things are passed away.' . . . And the twelve gates were twelve pearls, every several gate was one pearl; and the street of the city was fine gold, as it were transparent glass. And I saw no temple therein, for the Lord God Almighty and the Lamb are the temple of it. And the city had no need of the sun neither of the moon to shine in it, for the glory of God did lighten it, and the Lamb is the light thereof. And the nations shall walk in the light of it, and the kings of the earth do bring their glory into it. And the gates of it shall not be shut at all by day (for there shall be no night there). And they shall bring the glory and honour of the nations into it. And there shall in no wise enter into it anything that defileth, neither whatsoever worketh abomination or maketh a lie; but they which are written in the Lamb's Book of Life. . . . And there shall be no more curse; but the throne of the Lamb shall be therein; and His servants shall do Him service, and they shall see His face, and His name shall be on their foreheads. And there shall be no night there, and they need no candle, neither light of the sun, for the Lord God giveth them light, and they shall reign for ever and ever."

Here what is properly the action of the drama ends. What follows is an Epilogue, for it refers to the whole of the poem rather than to what imme- *Epilogue* diately precedes. The angel who has been the guide of the Seer assures him that the time of the Lord's coming, when all these things shall be fulfilled, is close at hand; and the Epilogue closes with one of those chorales, of which there are so many in the poem, which show the author's sense of harmony and power of orchestration: —

> "And the spirit and the Bride say, 'Come';
> And let him that heareth say, 'Come';
> And let him that is athirst come;
> And whosoever will, let him take the water
> Of life freely."

Finally the book closes with an *Envoi* or special address from the author to the reader, charging him to preserve the integrity of the book, and warning him again that the coming of the Lord is close at hand. To this is added the usual apostolic benediction and "Amen."

Envoi

The steps of the drama, then, are as follows: Act I, the Opening of the Seals of Fate; Act II, the Blowing of the Trumpets of Woe; Act III, the Establishment of the Kingdom of Heaven, and its Results; Act IV, the Judgment of the Earth, and of Rome; Act V, the Marriage of the Prince of Heaven, and the Glory of the Kingdom.

CHAPTER IV

THE END OF ALL THINGS

IT is interesting to study the difference between the eschatology of the Apocalypse and that of the Fourth Gospel and of St. Paul. The author of the Fourth Gospel holds that there will be a "last day," when there will be a resurrection of the just.[1] Whether this is the same as the general resurrection of just and unjust,[2] which is followed by the Judgment, is not certain. But all the facts of eschatology have a far more spiritual meaning given to them in the Fourth Gospel than in the Apocalypse. The material garment is barely sufficient, and is apparently regarded as hardly necessary to clothe the spiritual meaning. Identification with the spirit of Christ constitutes the resurrection.[3] Eternal life consists in the

[1] St. John vi. 39, 40; xi. 24.   [2] v. 28, 29.   [3] xi. 25, 26.

knowledge of Christ and of God. The Judgment is not so much an event taking place at a certain time in the future, as a continual, self-fulfilling process.[1] The rewards and punishments of that judgment are wholly devoid of even the appearance of arbitrariness, and are set forth as inherently necessary, because they are only a recognition of the existing condition of each man.

This is, it is true, by no means inconsistent with the view of the writer of the Apocalypse, who sees God seated on a great white throne, condemning this man to the lake of fire and brimstone and giving to that one a place in an everlasting kingdom. They are not logically antagonistic; both statements may mean the same thing. But it requires a certain degree of spiritual and intellectual growth to see that they mean the same. And it may be questioned whether, in that age, the mind capable of feeling strongly the scenic side of the end of the world could have felt also the inevitableness and inherent

[1] iii. 18, 19; xii. 47, 48.

nature of the causes which brought it about; for the points of view of poetry and of philosophy were diverse then as now.

In the eschatology of St. Paul no interval is fixed between the resurrection of the just and the general resurrection.[1] The duration of the reign of Christ is not given, and its character is exactly opposite to that mentioned in the Apocalypse. In the latter it is a time of uninterrupted happiness and peace, for Satan is bound and powerless, and the saints reign undisturbed on the earth. With St. Paul it is a time of unceasing warfare against hostile powers, and the duration of the period is limited by the time necessary for their complete subjugation.[2] The resurrection first of the just only, at the sound of the last of the trumpets (cf. 1 Cor. xv. 52, 54 with 1 Thess. iv. 16, 17), before all are raised, together with the victory that awaits them, would seem to imply an intervening reign of bliss; but no mention is made of a millennium, and the character given to the inter-

[1] 1 Thess. iv. 15–18. [2] 1 Cor. xv. 23–29.

vening period is militant and opposed to that of the millennium. Among all the New Testament writers, the thousand years' reign of bliss, the chaining and loosing of Satan, the attack of the heathen powers on the camp of the saints, and the victory of the forces of Heaven in battle are peculiar to the writer of the Apocalypse. It is a characteristic sign of the social condition of the world at the time, that the instrument of power, the means by which changes are to be brought about, is not legislation, education, nor growth, but an army.

Our outlook upon the future has so radically changed since the seventh or eighth century B.C. that it is difficult for us to understand the point of view of many of the prophets and psalmists of Israel. That there should be religious believers in annihilation for all men, such as, later, was the author of the Book of Ecclesiastes, does not puzzle us, for we see these still about us. But a belief which should regard the region beyond death as a sort of huge chamber in which all men are penned, existent indeed, but with no joys, no great pains, no hope, no outlook; a belief which should add to this, as time went on, the existence of a select few on earth with lives supernaturally prolonged, wielding a successful and beneficent government; a belief which should feel no rectification necessary of the disproportion between the lot of the few and that of the many — such a belief is foreign to us. And yet the Jew of the seventh or eighth century B.C. could feel no such disproportion, because he had so limited a sense of the value of the individual. The family, the tribe, the nation, organized life in some of its forms, these wholly filled his vision, and the individual as such had as against these no rights which could claim consideration. The sins of the fathers were to be visited on the children to the third and fourth generation. When Achan was condemned for what in the judgment of the day was treason, not only was he put to death, but with him "his sons and his daughters and his oxen and his asses and his sheep and his tent and all that he had."[1] It was not until the sixth century B.C. that a voice was raised against the traditional doctrine by Jeremiah from amid the ruins of Jerusalem. He declared that the sour grapes which the fathers had eaten should no more set on edge the children's teeth.[2] At almost the same time Ezekiel, too, in the midst of the hostile prosperity of Babylon, reiterated the lesson that corporate guilt or innocence did not supersede individual responsibility. "The soul that sinneth, *it* shall die."[3] Despair at the apparent failure of God's promises in regard to the nation led to the conviction that they must be individually fulfilled. And from this time the idea of corporate existence had a complement, which was never afterwards lost, in the idea of the individual. But the habit of mind of the thinker of the ancient world was to emphasize corporate relations. To him individuals were valuable for the sake of institutions; to us institutions are

---

[1] Josh. vii. 24, 25. [2] Jer. xxxi. 29, 30.
[3] Ezek. xviii. 4 f.

valuable for the sake of individuals. These are completely opposite points of view; and this must constantly be borne in mind in considering the Canaanitish wars, the Imprecatory Psalms, and the arguments of St. Paul as to the rejection of Israel and the adoption of the Gentiles. The Jew of the ninth century B.C. was in this respect at one extremity of a pole of thought, and we in the twentieth century A.D. are at the other. It is interesting to trace the gradations between the two; but it need only be noted here that in the Apocalypse there is a mingling of both elements. The Christian mind had come to demand a recognition in the future of the full personality of each human being; consequently in the vision of the Seer there was a resurrection of all the dead, small and great, standing before God. Sheol, the universal reception-chamber, opens its doors, and the sea gives back its dead. The latter were regarded as not having gone down to Sheol, another indication of the Hebrew ignorance and dread of the sea.[1] Each human being was

[1] Cf. p. 66.

unnecessary, even from the point of view which would regard its scheme as a final one. In the Apocalypse moral evil and its consequences are represented by physical pain. This, to many, has been a stumbling-block. They have not been able to reconcile it to their ideas of right that the wicked should be "cast into the lake of fire and brimstone." But this is certainly no more difficult to interpret than the statement of the writer that in Heaven there are Four composite Creatures, having eyes before and behind and within. Physical pain is a most useful representative of moral evil, and one which those who have to instruct immature minds still find it wise at times to employ. But whatever method of interpretation may be applied to the Apocalypse, there is no warrant for interpreting the everlasting torment of the wicked in one way and the Four Beasts and the sea of glass in another. If the former is actual, so must the latter be. If the latter are symbolical, so must be also the former. And their symbolic nature would imply not unreality, but reality. For every sign must have behind it something signified. If the lake of fire and brimstone and the sharp two-edged sword coming out of the mouth of the Lord are in any sense symbols, there must be an eternal reality behind them.

CHAPTER V

THE PERSON OF JESUS

THE last chapter of the Book of the Revelation brings before us a question, hints of which have been visible throughout the Book. The angel who has been the guide of the Seer hitherto, as the latter in his wonder and awe falls down before him, refuses his worship, professing to be one of the army of prophetic fellow-servants like himself, and bids him worship God. He goes on, however, to identify himself with Jesus, announcing that the time of his coming is at hand when he will judge the world. "I, Jesus," he says, "have sent mine $\mathring{α}γγελον$ [that is, the Seer] to testify unto you [that is, the audience of the Christian world] these things in the Churches. I am the root and offspring of

The Person of Jesus

David and the bright and morning star."[1] This is not the first time that Jesus has been regarded as an angel. In xi. 3 it is an angel who speaks; and yet the witnesses who are testifying to the Messiah's Kingdom he calls "my witnesses." Just after the Lamb has been mentioned, "another angel" is spoken of.[2] "The Son of Man," a title which elsewhere in the Book is applied to Jesus,[3] appears preceded by three angels and followed by three.[4] The frequency with which a band of angels consists of seven[5] would suggest that Jesus is regarded here as one, the chief, among them, even if the one who follows Him were not called "another angel."[6] The same speaker who refuses the Seer's worship, and bids him not to seal the prophetic Book, goes on to say, "Behold, I come quickly," and speaks of himself as the final Judge.[7]

It is evident, then, that in these passages

[1] xxii. 16. [2] xiv. 1, 4, 6. [3] i. 13. [4] xiv. 14.
[5] iv. 5; viii. 2; xv. 1. [6] xiv. 15. [7] xxii. 12, 13.

Jesus is regarded as having the nature of an angel, as the highest, the first created being. He is "the faithful and true witness, the beginning of the creation of God,"[1] just as to St. Paul He is "the firstborn of the whole creation."[2] He is "the Prince of the kings of the earth,"[3] who is exalted to a heavenly throne as a reward for His victorious conflicts.[4] But it was characteristic of the deepest spiritual insight and reverence of the author's time that it was coming to regard its dearly loved Master as joined in some unique way to the one Almighty God, as sharing His nature and rank. And so there rises to the prophet's lips the phrase descriptive of God, "The first and the last,"[5] which centuries earlier the great prophet of the Exile had used, and for which he, the Seer, had found as it recurred to his mind a fitting Greek symbol, "τὸ Ἄλφα καὶ τὸ Ὦ." This symbol he uses both of Jesus[6] and of God

[1] iii. 14. [2] Col. i. 15. [3] i. 5. [4] iii. 21. Cf. Phil. ii. 8, 9; Heb. ii. 9. [5] i. 17; xxii. 13. [6] xxii. 13.

Almighty,[1] feeling apparently no inconsistency in its double application. There are still other direct ascriptions to Jesus of the functions and attributes of God. And while we must beware of reading into them the metaphysical ideas which they connote to us, we cannot avoid seeing in them an association of Jesus with God which was possible in case of no other being. Thus, for example, He is the final Judge;[2] the receiver of supreme worship together with God;[3] the spirit of God;[4] the word of God;[5] the Son of God.[6] God and the Lamb occupy not two thrones, but one.[7] Throughout the poem the feelings with which Jesus is regarded are those of the deepest devotion and adoration, such as are aroused only by an object believed to be Divine.

The question then presents itself, What was the view of the author in regard to the

---

[1] i. 8, where cf. also Westcott and Hort's reading "κύριος ὁ θεός." The phrase in i. 11 is rejected as corrupt. The identification in ii. 16 is doubtful.

[2] i. 18; xxii. 12.   [3] v. 13; vii. 10; xxi. 22.   [4] ii. 7 f.
[5] xix. 13.   [6] ii. 18.   [7] v. 6; xxii. 1, 3.

mutual relations of God Almighty, of Jesus, and of the angel? The attempt has been made to avoid the inference that the angel in the last chapter identifies himself with Jesus by ascribing the different verses in it to different speakers. Thus vs. 6 is unquestionably spoken by the angel. But vs. 7, it is said, is not by the angel, because the speaker refers to the coming of the Lord as his own coming. Again, vss. 10, 11 belong to the angel, but 12, 13 to Jesus. 14, 15 are doubtful, but 16 is again that of Jesus. It is undoubtedly the case that the ancient Hebrew prophets in their impassioned dramatic utterances sometimes gave no indication of a change of speaker, putting their words now into the mouth of God, now speaking as from themselves, and now by the mouth of the people. The most usual instances of this are where the prophet alternates between words which he ascribes to God and those uttered in his own person.[1] In Isa. xxviii. 9–11, for example, in the midst of his own words, the

[1] Cf. Jer. xv. 8–19; xvii. 10–19.

prophet begins quoting the jeers of those who derided his preaching as commonplace and fit only for children. "Whom," they say, "shall he [the prophet] teach knowledge? and whom shall he make to understand a message? Them that are weaned from the milk and drawn from the breasts." It is not until a following verse that he shows plainly who it is into whose mouth he puts these words. It is "this people," to whom God said, "This is the rest wherewith ye may cause the weary to rest, and this is the refreshing, yet they would not hear." This is the prophet's stage-direction, as it were. But in the last chapter of the Book of the Revelation there are no stage-directions. And when commentators declare, what is undoubtedly true, that the context must determine the speaker, and then assume that because vss. 7, 12, 13, 16 refer unquestionably to Jesus they do not therefore refer to the angel, it is unwarrantably assuming the very point in question. Certainly the ordinary reader unwarned would never imagine a change of speaker to have taken place between vss. 6, 7 and 10, 12. It could occur to no one not preoccupied with the need of dogmatic harmonizing. This is precisely the attitude of mind most alien to that of the writer of the Apocalypse. From him, as already said, logical consistency in ideas and images and exclusiveness among them cannot be demanded. As he identifies Nero with one of the heads of the Beast, and then immediately, unconsciously, and with no sign of transition identifies him with the Beast as a whole, so here the highest angel and the beginning of the creation of God, the firstborn of every creature and the Prince of Heaven, the King of the new Kingdom and the eternal Judge, pass naturally and unconsciously into one another. If this seems strange, it can be so only to one who comes expecting to find everywhere the footprints of a carefully worked-out theological system, such as were those of the West. Such a system is not natural to the Oriental mind, and was foreign to the earliest days of Christianity. Valuable as such systems are, they are an adult growth, and in the history of Christianity it required several centuries and the influence of the West to produce them. Vision comes more naturally in the East than thought; and in a vision the images blend and pass into one another without condemning thereby the vision's genuineness or value.

The point of view of the Seer, then, is continually changing. He conceives of Jesus now as the highest of the creatures, now as the eternal beginning and end of all things. Our difficulty in comprehending this arises not only from the fact that to us each of these is a definite and separate conception, while to him such definiteness and separation did not exist; but also from the single idea conveyed to us by the word "angel" as compared with the double idea contained in the Greek ἄγγελος. To the Greek this word meant a messenger of any kind, as well as one of those beings whom we call distinctively angels. To speak of

Jesus as a divine ἄγγελος, then, would not be so foreign to the point of view which regarded Him as Son of God as to speak of Him as an "angel." But here again the Oriental mind, averse to minute distinctions of thought, would probably have found no difficulty where the Western mind might readily find one.

It is worthy of note that while the angel, Jesus, and God are at times regarded as separate beings and at times identified, the bond between them which allows their identification is a transcendent, spiritual one, an internal unity of character and function. This bond is similar to that which in the Fourth Gospel is asserted to exist among Jesus, His disciples, the Holy Spirit, and God. The spirit of Jesus is not merely to come into the world, but is to dwell with His disciples and to be in them; and the union among them, Himself, and God is inherent in the nature of spiritual life. "That they all may be one," He prays, "as Thou, Father, art in me and I in Thee, that they also may be one in us."[1] It is this recognition of the true nature of the bond between Christ and His own that is the special characteristic of the Fourth Gospel. The author has apprehended, as has hardly any one else, hardly even St. Paul, the fact that the believer is joined to Christ through being filled with a spirit like His; or rather, since that would imply many distinct spirits of one and the same kind, and since spirit is in reality not individual but universal, it is through being filled with Christ's spirit, through sharing with Him in a common spiritual life. To the other Evangelists the relations between Christ and those who are His are largely material and external. He is to take them to His Heavenly Kingdom; they are to possess the earth. His apostles shall sit on twelve thrones and judge the twelve tribes of Israel. But while to the Fourth Evangelist, as to the others, there was no sharp line of division between material and spiritual, form and essence, with

[1] St. John xvii. 21.

him the spiritual had a higher range and wider inclusiveness. It is this that gives him his penetrating view into the essential nature of the resurrection and eternal life.[1] It is this that reveals to him the secret of Christ's marvellous power in His profound God-consciousness.[2] And it is this depth and intensity of spiritual gaze rather than the dogmatic character of its discourses, which have made the Fourth Gospel dear to the Christian heart.

The difference in mode of treatment of the same subjects in the Apocalypse and the Fourth Gospel is suggestive as showing points of view not so much opposed as developed more or less fully. The Apocalypse is the earlier book, both historically and logically, and was a necessary step toward the capacity of spiritual apprehension which the Fourth Gospel shows. "In the Apocalypse," says Dr. Westcott, "the thought is of an outward coming for the open judgment of men; in the Gospel, of a

[1] St. John xi. 25, 26; xvii. 3.   [2] iv. 34; x. 28–31.

judgment which is spiritual and self-executing. In the Apocalypse the scene of the consummation is a renovated world; in the Gospel, the Father's House. In the former the victory and the transformation are from without, by might, and the 'future' is painted in historic imagery; in the latter, the victory and the transformation are from within, by a spiritual influence, and the 'future' is present and eternal. In a word, the study of the Synoptists, of the Apocalypse, and of the Gospel of St. John in succession, enables us to see under what human conditions the full majesty of Christ was perceived and declared, not all at once, but step by step, and by the help of the old prophetic teaching."

That the author of the Apocalypse identified Jesus with the highest angel may be a fact of much significance or of little. Of much, if created limitation was the side accented in the author's mind, if a distinctively angelic character and functions are assigned to Him; of little, if this was merely one point of view among many, and if there are ascribed to Him the mediatorial, redemptive, and essentially Divine characteristics which the Christian Church through the centuries has insisted must form part of the highest and truest view of Jesus. If we remember that Jesus is apparently identified with the angel, we must also remember that He is as apparently identified with the Supreme God. If we then insist upon logical exactitude of thought, the Apocalypse will have nothing to say to us. The demand, "He must be regarded as either the one or the other. Which is it?" the inspired Seer would probably have been unable to understand.

Other instances of this characteristic of thought and style, which leads the author to interchange predicates and regard the same objects in various lights, are the following: The final Judge is at one time declared to be God and at another Christ.[1] It is said there will be a complete renovation

[1] Cf. xx. 12; xxi. 4 with xxii. 12; vi. 16, 17.

of both Heaven and earth.[1] And yet various classes of sinners who remain from the old condition of things are represented as having their permanent abode outside the heavenly city;[2] and this though they have already been consigned to the lake of fire and brimstone.[3] The relations of Jew and Gentile are also regarded with inconsistency. On the one hand, they form one community without distinction, and both alike are kings and priests unto God.[4] Sonship to God is conditioned on moral character, not on ancestry.[5] The water of life is for whosoever will.[6] And yet, on the other hand, between Jew and Gentile there is an indelible distinction. The firstfruits of the Messiah's Kingdom are the nation of Israel in its ideal estate,[7] while the saved Gentiles are set in contrast with them,[8] and are even not mentioned as belonging to the redeemed.[9] The Kingdom of Christ is built on a distinctively Jewish model. It is not

[1] xxi. 1. [2] xxii. 15. [3] xxi. 8. [4] i. 6; v. 10.
[5] xxi. 7. [6] xxii. 17. [7] vii. 4–9. [8] vii. 9.
[9] xiv. 1, 3.

only that it is regarded as Jerusalem made new, but every one who enters must come in through one of twelve gates, each of which represents one of the tribes of Israel.[1] The fruit of the tree of life is designed for Israelites, for there are twelve kinds of it, while for the Gentiles there are only its leaves for healing purposes.[2] Such inconsistencies would have seemed to the author and to every Oriental mind to involve no breach of thought nor detraction from the worth of the literary work in which they occurred.

[1] xxi. 12.   [2] xxii. 2.

CHAPTER VI

THE LITERARY VALUE OF THE APOCALYPSE

APOCALYPSES were a favorite form of literature in times when the outlook was dark and the glow of original prophetic genius was dim. Their object was to encourage and comfort by holding out the hope of speedy deliverance. Much as the later Jewish and early Christian literature was in this form, and the masterpieces of former ages influenced profoundly the author of the Book of the Revelation. For example, the details of the new Jerusalem, the measuring of the city, the river of life, the ever-fruitful tree, are taken from Ezekiel, though their roots are earlier still, and in the New Testament more of spiritual significance is infused into them. The beasts with many heads and horns, the measuring of time by the prophetic week, the name "Son of Man," and the appearance of the Ancient of Days are found also in Daniel. Among other apocalypses which formed part of the later Jewish literature are the following: Ethiopic Enoch, dating 200–95 B.C.; the Testaments of the Twelve Patriarchs, second and first centuries B.C.; the Psalms of Solomon, 70–40 B.C.; the Fourth Book of Ezra, perhaps 97 A.D.; the Book of Jubilees, or the Little Genesis, the first quarter of the first century A.D.; the Assumption of Moses, the same date; the Apocalypse of Baruch, the latter half of the first century. Among Christian apocalypses of this period are the Apocalypse of Esdras, belonging to the second or third century A.D.; the Ascension and Vision of Isaiah, the same date; the Apocalypse of Paul, late in the fourth century; the Apocalypse of John, not earlier than the fifth century.

As the years went by and the Lord's Kingdom did not appear upon earth; as devout believers had to meet not only the jeers of their opponents, but the harrowing doubt of their own minds, — "Where is the promise of His coming? For since the fathers fell asleep, all things continue as they were from the beginning of the creation," — as the world went on its course, giving no sign of any fulfilment of their hopes; men, on the one hand, settled down into the conviction that the Kingdom of Christ was represented in the Church, — a conviction established on a firm basis by Augustine in his *De Civitate Dei*, — and, on the other hand, they endeavored to galvanize into new life the primitive faith, in spite of apparent contradiction. This attempt was begun by Montanism in the second century, and continued in various forms of Millenarianism to our own day. Montanism was the first of the many Christian attempts to reform the world by the endeavor to restore conditions which were assumed to be primitive. Like so many other similar attempts, it was the expression of a noble protest, a protest against the tendency of the Church to strike a bargain with the world and arrange herself comfortably in it. As the hold of the Church, however, became firmly established, expectation of an upheaval, even of an upheaval with Christ at its head, died away. For the expectation of Millenarianism was not of a kingdom which should be the consummation of a process of evolution and development of the Church, but a special implanting of the glory of the hereafter into the imperfections of this world. When the Protestant Reformation thrilled men with vague and infinite hopes, it seemed as if all things were about to be made new, and the millennial kingdom of Christ would immediately appear. As, however, in the first half of the Book of the Revelation, the *dénoûment* of the drama is continually postponed, so in the history of the world, the ultimate moment, always on the point of happening, never arrives; the bright vision recedes, and life drops back into its old humdrum ways. Yet still those who are tied to literalism in exegesis, those whose world is so bad that they cannot endure it without hope of a speedy deliverance, those who see no reason why God should not do anything they wish, these have been ever inclined to fix the place and the hour when Christ would descend through the clouds, and by a mighty convulsion transform the world into His Kingdom. The Irvingites in England in 1831, the Millerites in New England in 1843, the Mormons in their exodus to Utah in 1847, are instances of religious movements in the last century in which the expectation of an earthly kingdom played a prominent part.

It would seem as if the strenuous exertions which the author of the Apocalypse made to impress upon his readers that the end of all things was only a few years distant, might have preserved his book from the exegetical fate which has befallen it. For there has never perhaps been a work which has received more divergent interpretations and more fantastic ones. During the first three centuries the general meaning of the Book was preserved — the knowledge that it took its rise in the conditions of the middle of the first century, that it reflected those conditions, and that it was designed by its author to apply to the present and the near future. But when the Church came to be united with the Empire, the ecclesiastical authorities of the time could not recognize the inspiration and canonicity of a book whose main burden was hatred of Rome and prediction of her downfall. They consequently tried to destroy its prestige by declaring it apocryphal. But it had made itself too strong a place in the mind and affections of the Christian world to be uprooted. Attempts were then made, by fanciful exegesis, to explain away allusions which were objectionable. The condition of the science of Biblical interpretation made such attempts natural and easy; for the aim of exegesis then was not so much to discover what meaning the text actually had, as what meaning it might with edification have. Toward the twelfth century, when the traditions of the early Fathers had less weight, all historical basis for the Book was forgotten, and it was directly transferred to the province of poetic fancy. That was declared to belong to the remote future which its author had distinctly asserted to refer to a period but a few years distant from the time at which he wrote. The custom of identifying the spiritual enemies denounced in the Book with existing heretics and schismatics began in the thirteenth century. Pope Innocent III affirmed the Saracens to be the true Antichrist, Mohammed the False Prophet, and 666 years the duration of his power. After the Reformation the Pope himself became Antichrist, or, by a different interpretation, the Beast was the line of Popes. On the other hand, the star which fell from Heaven has within a century been identified with Luther, who renounced his faith and thus fell. It has also been confidently announced that the Beast was Napoleon Bonaparte.

All such attempts leave the Book what they found it, — a riddle composed of many bits, each bit to be fitted into place here and there along the centuries by ingenious guessing. For this, as well as every other book, must be found a riddle by any exegesis which does not endeavor to ascertain, first what the work in question meant to the author and his time, and secondly, what power of instruction and encouragement it has for men of all time. Its function in giving information as to past events or those yet to come will always be subordinate. The second of these considerations will determine worth, determine whether or not a book has "inspiration," or, more properly, the power of inspiring.

Such inspiration in the Apocalypse was recognized not only by early ages, but has been recognized by all ages succeeding. Not that power of inspiring which is felt in the loftier Psalms and the Restoration Epic of the Old Testament, or the Gospels and Pauline Epistles of the New, for the spiritual standpoint of the Apocalypse is distinctly lower than these. But its value lies in the certainty of the author's conviction of the ultimate triumph of righteousness, the sternness of his hatred of evil-doers, the gorgeousness of his imagination, his sense of harmony, the harmony of mighty voices filled with pure and passionate feeling, and the more subtle harmonies which can be heard only with the ear of the soul. What it has done, it can do; and it has stirred men's souls and raised them to the throne of God. It has made them feel disaster, failure, persecution, to be matters of little account. It has sent them singing to their deaths with a vivid realization of glory before them. It has comforted those who were hard pressed with the thought that it was but for a little while. It has expressed spiritual realities in concrete terms, so that the child and the ignorant man could grasp them. And it has tinged the thought of the world, so that not only the language of devotion, but that of common life has become colored by it. It is the last great prophecy of the spirit of Israel, the first poem of Christianity.

CHAPTER VII

THE REVELATION OF ST. JOHN THE DIVINE

(Revised Version, 1881)

1 THE Revelation of Jesus Christ, which God gave him to shew unto his servants, even the things which must shortly come to pass: and he sent and signified it by his angel unto his
2 servant John; who bare witness of the word of God, and of the testimony of Jesus Christ, even of all things that
3 he saw. Blessed is he that readeth, and they that hear the words of the prophecy, and keep the things which are written therein: for the time is at hand.

4 JOHN to the seven churches which are in Asia: Grace to you and peace, from him which is and which was and which

is to come; and from the seven Spirits
5 which are before his throne; and from
Jesus Christ, who is the faithful witness,
the firstborn of the dead, and the ruler
of the kings of the earth. Unto him
that loveth us, and loosed us from our
6 sins by his blood; and he made us to
be a kingdom, to be priests unto his
God and Father; to him be the glory and
the dominion for ever and ever. Amen.
7 Behold, he cometh with the clouds; and
every eye shall see him, and they which
pierced him; and all the tribes of the
earth shall mourn over him. Even so,
Amen.
8 I am the Alpha and the Omega, saith
the Lord God, which is and which was
and which is to come, the Almighty.
9 I John, your brother and partaker with
you in the tribulation and kingdom and
patience which were in Jesus, was in the
isle that is called Patmos, for the word
10 of God and the testimony of Jesus. I
was in the Spirit on the Lord's day, and

I heard behind me a great voice, as of a trumpet saying, What thou seest, write in a book, and send it to the seven churches; unto Ephesus, and unto Smyrna, and unto Pergamum, and unto Thyatira, and unto Sardis, and unto Philadelphia, and unto Laodicea. And I turned to see the voice which spake with me. And having turned I saw seven golden candlesticks; and in the midst of the candlesticks one like unto a son of man, clothed with a garment down to the foot, and girt about at the breasts with a golden girdle. And his head and his hair were white as white wool, white as snow; and his eyes were as a flame of fire; and his feet like unto burnished brass, as if it had been refined in a furnace; and his voice as the voice of many waters. And he had in his right hand seven stars: and out of his mouth proceeded a sharp two-edged sword: and his countenance was as the sun shineth in his strength. And when

I saw him, I fell at his feet as one dead. And he laid his right hand upon me, 18 saying, Fear not; I am the first and the last, and the Living one; and I was dead, and behold, I am alive for evermore, and I have the keys of death and 19 of Hades. Write therefore the things which thou sawest, and the things which are, and the things which shall come to 20 pass hereafter; the mystery of the seven stars which thou sawest in my right hand, and the seven golden candlesticks. The seven stars are the angels of the seven churches: and the seven candlesticks are seven churches.

2 To the angel of the church in Ephesus write;

These things saith he that holdeth the seven stars in his right hand, he that walketh in the midst of the seven golden 2 candlesticks: I know thy works, and thy toil and patience, and that thou canst not bear evil men, and didst try them which call themselves apostles, and they are not,

3 and didst find them false; and thou hast patience and didst bear for my name's
4 sake, and hast not grown weary. But I have this against thee, that thou didst
5 leave thy first love. Remember therefore from whence thou art fallen, and repent, and do the first works; or else I come to thee, and will move thy candlestick out of its place, except thou repent.
6 But this thou hast, that thou hatest the works of the Nicolaitans, which I also
7 hate. He that hath an ear, let him hear what the Spirit saith to the churches. To him that overcometh, to him will I give to eat of the tree of life, which is in the Paradise of God.

8 And to the angel of the church in Smyrna write;

These things saith the first and the last,
9 which was dead, and lived again: I know thy tribulation, and thy poverty (but thou art rich), and the blasphemy of them which say they are Jews, and they are
10 not, but are a synagogue of Satan. Fear

not the things which thou art about to suffer: behold, the devil is about to cast some of you into prison, that ye may be tried; and ye shall have tribulation ten days. Be thou faithful unto death, and I 11 will give thee the crown of life. He that hath an ear, let him hear what the Spirit saith to the churches. He that overcometh shall not be hurt of the second death.

12 And to the angel of the church in Pergamum write;

These things saith he that hath the 13 sharp two-edged sword: I know where thou dwellest, even where Satan's throne is: and thou holdest fast my name, and didst not deny my faith, even in the days of Antipas my witness, my faithful one, who was killed among you, where Satan 14 dwelleth. But I have a few things against thee, because thou hast there some that hold the teaching of Balaam, who taught Balak to cast a stumblingblock before the children of Israel, to eat things sacrificed 15 to idols, and to commit fornication. So

hast thou also some that hold the teaching of the Nicolaitans in like manner.
16 Repent therefore; or else I come to thee quickly, and I will make war against
17 them with the sword of my mouth. He that hath an ear, let him hear what the Spirit saith to the churches. To him that overcometh, to him will I give of the hidden manna, and I will give him a white stone, and upon the stone a new name written, which no one knoweth but he that receiveth it.

18 And to the angel of the church in Thyatira write;

These things saith the Son of God, who hath his eyes like a flame of fire, and his
19 feet are like unto burnished brass: I know thy works, and thy love and faith and ministry and patience, and that thy
20 last works are more than the first. But I have this against thee, that thou sufferest the woman Jezebel, which calleth herself a prophetess; and she teacheth and seduceth my servants to commit for-

nication, and to eat things sacrificed to
21 idols. And I gave her time that she
should repent; and she willeth not to
22 repent of her fornication. Behold, I do
cast her into a bed, and them that commit adultery with her into great tribulation, except they repent of her works.
23 And I will kill her children with death;
and all the churches shall know that I
am he which searcheth the reins and
hearts: and I will give unto each one of
24 you according to your works. But to you
I say, to the rest that are in Thyatira, as
many as have not this teaching, which
know not the deep things of Satan, as
they say; I cast upon you none other
25 burden. Howbeit that which ye have,
26 hold fast till I come. And he that overcometh, and he that keepeth my works
unto the end, to him will I give authority
27 over the nations: and he shall rule them
with a rod of iron, as the vessels of the
potter are broken to shivers; as I also
28 have received of my Father: and I will

29 give him the morning star. He that hath an ear, let him hear what the Spirit saith to the churches.

3 And to the angel of the church in Sardis write;

These things saith he that hath the seven Spirits of God, and the seven stars: I know thy works, that thou hast a name that thou livest, and thou art
2 dead. Be thou watchful, and stablish the things that remain, which were ready to die: for I have found no works of
3 thine fulfilled before my God. Remember therefore how thou hast received and didst hear; and keep it, and repent. If therefore thou shalt not watch, I will come as a thief, and thou shalt not know
4 what hour I will come upon thee. But thou hast a few names in Sardis which did not defile their garments: and they shall walk with me in white; for they are
5 worthy. He that overcometh shall thus be arrayed in white garments; and I will in no wise blot his name out of the book

of life, and I will confess his name before
6 my Father, and before his angels. He that hath an ear, let him hear what the Spirit saith to the churches.

7 And to the angel of the church in Philadelphia write;

These things saith he that is holy, he that is true, he that hath the key of David, he that openeth, and none shall shut, and that shutteth, and none open-
8 eth: I know thy works (behold, I have set before thee a door opened, which none can shut), that thou hast a little power, and didst keep my word, and didst not
9 deny my name. Behold, I give of the synagogue of Satan, of them which say they are Jews, and they are not, but do lie; behold, I will make them to come and worship before thy feet, and to know
10 that I have loved thee. Because thou didst keep the word of my patience, I also will keep thee from the hour of trial, that hour which is to come upon the whole world, to try them that dwell upon

11 the earth. I come quickly: hold fast that which thou hast, that no one take thy
12 crown. He that overcometh, I will make him a pillar in the temple of my God, and he shall go out thence no more: and I will write upon him the name of my God, and the name of the city of my God, the new Jerusalem, which cometh down out of heaven from my God, and mine
13 own new name. He that hath an ear, let him hear what the Spirit saith to the churches.

14 And to the angel of the church in Laodicea write;

These things saith the Amen, the faithful and true witness, the beginning of the
15 creation of God: I know thy works, that thou art neither cold nor hot: I would
16 thou wert cold or hot. So because thou art lukewarm, and neither hot nor cold, I
17 will spew thee out of my mouth. Because thou sayest, I am rich, and have gotten riches, and have need of nothing; and knowest not that thou art the wretched

one and miserable and poor and blind
18 and naked: I counsel thee to buy of me
gold refined by fire, that thou mayest become rich; and white garments, that thou
mayest clothe thyself, and that the shame
of thy nakedness be not made manifest;
and eyesalve to anoint thine eyes, that
19 thou mayest see. As many as I love, I
reprove and chasten: be zealous therefore,
20 and repent. Behold, I stand at the door
and knock: if any man hear my voice and
open the door, I will come in to him, and
21 will sup with him, and he with me. He
that overcometh, I will give to him to sit
down with me in my throne, as I also
overcame, and sat down with my Father
22 in his throne. He that hath an ear, let
him hear what the Spirit saith to the
churches.

4 After these things I saw, and behold,
a door opened in heaven, and the first
voice which I heard, a voice as of a trumpet speaking with me, one saying, Come
up hither, and I will shew thee the things

which must come to pass hereafter.
2 Straightway I was in the Spirit: and behold, there was a throne set in heaven,
3 and one sitting upon the throne; and he that sat was to look upon like a jasper stone and a sardius: and there was a rainbow round about the throne, like an
4 emerald to look upon. And round about the throne were four and twenty thrones: and upon the thrones I saw four and twenty elders sitting, arrayed in white garments; and on their heads crowns of
5 gold. And out of the throne proceed lightnings and voices and thunders. And there were seven lamps of fire burning before the throne, which are the seven
6 Spirits of God; and before the throne, as it were a glassy sea like unto crystal; and in the midst of the throne, and round about the throne, four living creatures
7 full of eyes before and behind. And the first creature was like a lion, and the second creature like a calf, and the third creature had a face as of a man, and the

fourth creature was like a flying eagle.
8 And the four living creatures, having each one of them six wings, are full of eyes round about and within: and they have no rest day and night, saying, Holy, holy, holy, is the Lord God, the Almighty, which was and which is and which is
9 to come. And when the living creatures shall give glory and honour and thanks to him that sitteth on the throne, to him
10 that liveth for ever and ever, the four and twenty elders shall fall down before him that sitteth on the throne, and shall worship him that liveth for ever and ever, and shall cast their crowns before
11 the throne, saying, Worthy art thou, our Lord and our God, to receive the glory and the honour and the power: for thou didst create all things, and because of thy will they were, and were created.

5 And I saw in the right hand of him that sat on the throne a book written within and on the back, close sealed with seven

2 seals. And I saw a strong angel proclaiming with a great voice, Who is worthy to open the book, and to loose
3 the seals thereof? And no one in the heaven, or on the earth, or under the earth, was able to open the book, or to
4 look thereon. And I wept much, because no one was found worthy to open the
5 book, or to look thereon: and one of the elders saith unto me, Weep not: behold, the Lion that is of the tribe of Judah, the Root of David, hath overcome, to open the book and the seven seals thereof.
6 And I saw in the midst of the throne and of the four living creatures, and in the midst of the elders, a Lamb standing, as though it had been slain, having seven horns, and seven eyes, which are the seven
7 Spirits of God, sent forth into all the earth. And he came, and he taketh it out
8 of the right hand of him that sat on the throne. And when he had taken the book, the four living creatures and the four and twenty elders fell down before the Lamb,

having each one a harp, and golden bowls full of incense, which are the prayers of the
9 saints. And they sing a new song, saying, Worthy art thou to take the book, and to open the seals thereof: for thou wast slain, and didst purchase unto God with thy blood men of every tribe, and
10 tongue, and people, and nation, and madest them to be unto our God a kingdom and priests; and they reign upon the
11 earth. And I saw, and I heard a voice of many angels round about the throne and the living creatures and the elders; and the number of them was ten thousand times ten thousand, and thousands of
12 thousands; saying with a great voice, Worthy is the Lamb that hath been slain to receive the power, and riches, and wisdom, and might, and honour, and glory,
13 and blessing. And every created thing which is in the heaven, and on the earth, and under the earth, and on the sea, and all things that are in them, heard I saying, Unto him that sitteth on the throne, and

unto the Lamb, be the blessing, and the honour, and the glory, and the dominion,
14 for ever and ever. And the four living creatures said, Amen. And the elders fell down and worshipped.

6 And I saw when the Lamb opened one of the seven seals, and I heard one of the four living creatures saying as with a
2 voice of thunder, Come. And I saw, and behold, a white horse, and he that sat thereon had a bow; and there was given unto him a crown: and he came forth conquering, and to conquer.

3 And when he opened the second seal, I heard the second living creature saying,
4 Come. And another horse came forth, a red horse: and to him that sat thereon it was given to take peace from the earth, and that they should slay one another: and there was given unto him a great sword.

5 And when he opened the third seal, I heard the third living creature saying, Come. And I saw, and behold, a black

horse; and he that sat thereon had a
6 balance in his hand. And I heard as it were a voice in the midst of the four living creatures, saying, A measure of wheat for a penny, and three measures of barley for a penny; and the oil and the wine hurt thou not.

7 And when he opened the fourth seal, I heard the voice of the fourth living crea-
8 ture saying, Come. And I saw, and behold, a pale horse: and he that sat upon him, his name was Death; and Hades followed with him. And there was given unto them authority over the fourth part of the earth, to kill with sword, and with famine, and with death, and by the wild beasts of the earth.

9 And when he opened the fifth seal, I saw underneath the altar the souls of them that had been slain for the word of God, and for the testimony which they
10 held: and they cried with a great voice, saying, How long, O Master, the holy and true, dost thou not judge and avenge

our blood on them that dwell on the
11 earth? And there was given them to each one a white robe; and it was said unto them, that they should rest yet for a little time, until their fellow-servants also and their brethren, which should be killed even as they were, should be fulfilled.
12 And I saw when he opened the sixth seal, and there was a great earthquake; and the sun became black as sackcloth of hair, and the whole moon became as
13 blood; and the stars of the heaven fell unto the earth, as a fig tree casteth her unripe figs, when she is shaken of a great
14 wind. And the heaven was removed as a scroll when it is rolled up; and every mountain and island were moved out of
15 their places. And the kings of the earth, and the princes, and the chief captains, and the rich, and the strong, and every bondman and freeman, hid themselves in the caves and in the rocks of the moun-
16 tains; and they say to the mountains and to the rocks, Fall on us, and hide us from

the face of him that sitteth on the throne,
17 and from the wrath of the Lamb: for the great day of their wrath is come; and who is able to stand?

7 After this I saw four angels standing at the four corners of the earth, holding the four winds of the earth, that no wind should blow on the earth, or on the sea,
2 or upon any tree. And I saw another angel ascend from the sunrising, having the seal of the living God: and he cried with a great voice to the four angels, to whom it was given to hurt the earth and
3 the sea, saying, Hurt not the earth, neither the sea, nor the trees, till we shall have sealed the servants of our God
4 on their foreheads. And I heard the number of them which were sealed, a hundred and forty and four thousand, sealed out of every tribe of the children of Israel.

5 Of the tribe of Judah were sealed twelve thousand:

Of the tribe of Reuben twelve thousand:

Of the tribe of Gad twelve thousand:
6 Of the tribe of Asher twelve thousand:
Of the tribe of Naphtali twelve thousand:
Of the tribe of Manasseh twelve thousand:
7 Of the tribe of Simeon twelve thousand:
Of the tribe of Levi twelve thousand:
Of the tribe of Issachar twelve thousand:
8 Of the tribe of Zebulun twelve thousand:
Of the tribe of Joseph twelve thousand:
Of the tribe of Benjamin were sealed twelve thousand.
9 After these things I saw, and behold, a great multitude, which no man could number, out of every nation, and of all tribes and peoples and tongues, standing before the throne and before the Lamb, arrayed in white robes, and palms in their
10 hands; and they cry with a great voice,

saying, Salvation unto our God which sitteth on the thone, and unto the Lamb.
11 And all the angels were standing round about the throne, and about the elders and the four living creatures; and they fell before the throne on their faces, and
12 worshipped God, saying, Amen: Blessing, and glory, and wisdom, and thanksgiving, and honour, and power, and might, be unto our God for ever and
13 ever. Amen. And one of the elders answered, saying unto me, These which are arrayed in the white robes, who are
14 they, and whence came they? And I say unto him, My lord, thou knowest. And he said to me, These are they which come out of the great tribulation, and they washed their robes, and made them
15 white in the blood of the Lamb. Therefore are they before the throne of God; and they serve him day and night in his temple: and he that sitteth on the throne shall spread his tabernacle over them.
16 They shall hunger no more, neither

thirst any more; neither shall the sun
17 strike upon them, nor any heat: for the
Lamb which is in the midst of the throne
shall be their shepherd, and shall guide
them unto fountains of waters of life:
and God shall wipe away every tear from
their eyes.

8 And when he opened the seventh seal,
there followed a silence in heaven about
2 the space of half an hour. And I saw
the seven angels which stand before
God; and there were given unto them
seven trumpets.

3 And another angel came and stood
over the altar, having a golden censer;
and there was given unto him much incense, that he should add it unto the
prayers of all the saints upon the golden
4 altar which was before the throne. And
the smoke of the incense, with the prayers
of the saints, went up before God out of
5 the angel's hand. And the angel taketh
the censer; and he filled it with the fire
of the altar, and cast it upon the earth:

and there followed thunders, and voices, and lightnings, and an earthquake.

6 And the seven angels which had the seven trumpets prepared themselves to sound.

7 And the first sounded, and there followed hail and fire, mingled with blood, and they were cast upon the earth: and the third part of the earth was burnt up, and the third part of the trees was burnt up, and all green grass was burnt up.

8 And the second angel sounded, and as it were a great mountain burning with fire was cast into the sea; and the third part
9 of the sea became blood; and there died the third part of the creatures which were in the sea, even they that had life; and the third part of the ships was destroyed.

10 And the third angel sounded, and there fell from heaven a great star, burning as a torch, and it fell upon the third part of the rivers, and upon the fountains of the
11 waters; and the name of the star is called Wormwood: and the third part of the

waters became wormwood; and many men died of the waters, because they were made bitter.

12 And the fourth angel sounded, and the third part of the sun was smitten, and the third part of the moon, and the third part of the stars; that the third part of them should be darkened, and the day should not shine for the third part of it, and the night in like manner.

13 And I saw, and I heard an eagle, flying in mid heaven, saying with a great voice, Woe, woe, woe, for them that dwell on the earth, by reason of the other voices of the trumpet of the three angels, who are yet to sound.

9 And the fifth angel sounded, and I saw a star from heaven fallen unto the earth: and there was given to him the key of
2 the pit of the abyss. And he opened the pit of the abyss; and there went up a smoke out of the pit, as the smoke of a great furnace; and the sun and the air were darkened by reason of the smoke of

3 the pit. And out of the smoke came forth locusts upon the earth; and power was given them, as the scorpions of the
4 earth have power. And it was said unto them that they should not hurt the grass of the earth, neither any green thing, neither any tree, but only such men as have not
5 the seal of God on their foreheads. And it was given them that they should not kill them, but that they should be tormented five months: and their torment was as the torment of a scorpion, when it
6 striketh a man. And in those days men shall seek death, and shall in no wise find it; and they shall desire to die, and death
7 fleeth from them. And the shapes of the locusts were like unto horses prepared for war; and upon their heads as it were crowns like unto gold, and their
8 faces were as men's faces. And they had hair as the hair of women, and their teeth
9 were as the teeth of lions. And they had breastplates, as it were breastplates of iron; and the sound of their wings was

as the sound of chariots, of many horses
10 rushing to war. And they have tails like unto scorpions, and stings; and in their tails is their power to hurt men five
11 months. They have over them as king the angel of the abyss: his name in Hebrew is Abaddon, and in the Greek tongue he hath the name Apollyon.

12 The first Woe is past: behold, there come yet two Woes hereafter.

13 And the sixth angel sounded, and I heard a voice from the horns of the
14 golden altar which is before God, one saying to the sixth angel, which had the trumpet, Loose the four angels which are
15 bound at the great river Euphrates. And the four angels were loosed, which had been prepared for the hour and day and month and year, that they should kill the
16 third part of men. And the number of the armies of the horsemen was twice ten thousand times ten thousand: I heard the
17 number of them. And thus I saw the horses in the vision, and them that sat on

them, having breastplates as of fire and of hyacinth and of brimstone: and the heads of the horses are as the heads of lions; and out of their mouths proceed-
18 eth fire and smoke and brimstone. By these three plagues was the third part of men killed, by the fire and the smoke and the brimstone, which proceeded out
19 of their mouths. For the power of the horses is in their mouth, and in their tails: for their tails are like unto serpents, and have heads; and with them they do
20 hurt. And the rest of mankind, which were not killed with these plagues, repented not of the works of their hands, that they should not worship devils, and the idols of gold, and of silver, and of brass, and of stone, and of wood; which
21 can neither see, nor hear, nor walk: and they repented not of their murders, nor of their sorceries, nor of their fornication, nor of their thefts.

10 And I saw another strong angel coming down out of heaven, arrayed with a cloud;

and the rainbow was upon his head, and
his face was as the sun, and his feet as
2 pillars of fire; and he had in his hand
a little book open: and he set his right
foot upon the sea, and his left upon the
3 earth; and he cried with a great voice, as
a lion roareth: and when he cried, the
4 seven thunders uttered their voices. And
when the seven thunders uttered their
voices, I was about to write: and I heard
a voice from heaven saying, Seal up the
things which the seven thunders uttered,
5 and write them not. And the angel
which I saw standing upon the sea and
upon the earth lifted up his right hand to
6 heaven, and sware by him that liveth for
ever and ever, who created the heaven
and the things that are therein, and the
earth and the things that are therein, and
the sea and the things that are therein, that
7 there shall be time no longer: but in the
days of the voice of the seventh angel,
when he is about to sound, then is finished
the mystery of God, according to the good

tidings which he declared to his servants
8 the prophets. And the voice which I
heard from heaven, I heard it again speaking with me, and saying, Go, take the book
which is open in the hand of the angel
that standeth upon the sea and upon the
9 earth. And I went unto the angel, saying
unto him that he should give me the little
book. And he saith unto me, Take it,
and eat it up; and it shall make thy belly
bitter, but in thy mouth it shall be sweet
10 as honey. And I took the little book out
of the angel's hand, and ate it up; and it
was in my mouth sweet as honey: and
when I had eaten it, my belly was made
11 bitter. And they say unto me, Thou
must prophesy again over many peoples
and nations and tongues and kings.

11 And there was given me a reed like
unto a rod; and one said, Rise, and
measure the temple of God, and the
altar, and them that worship therein.
2 And the court which is without the
temple leave without, and measure it

not; for it hath been given unto the nations: and the holy city shall they tread under foot forty and two months.
3 And I will give unto my two witnesses, and they shall prophesy a thousand two hundred and threescore days, clothed
4 in sackcloth. These are the two olive trees and the two candlesticks, standing
5 before the Lord of the earth. And if any man desireth to hurt them, fire proceedeth out of their mouth, and devoureth their enemies: and if any man shall desire to hurt them, in this manner
6 must he be killed. These have the power to shut the heaven, that it rain not during the days of their prophecy: and they have power over the waters to turn them into blood, and to smite the earth with every plague, as often as they
7 shall desire. And when they shall have finished their testimony, the beast that cometh up out of the abyss shall make
8 war with them, and overcome them, and kill them. And their dead bodies lie

in the street of the great city, which spiritually is called Sodom and Egypt, where also their Lord was crucified. 9 And from among the peoples and tribes and tongues and nations do men look upon their dead bodies three days and a half, and suffer not their dead bodies to 10 be laid in a tomb. And they that dwell on the earth rejoice over them, and make merry; and they shall send gifts one to another; because these two prophets tormented them that dwell on the earth. 11 And after the three days and a half the breath of life from God entered into them, and they stood upon their feet; and great fear fell upon them which be-12 held them. And they heard a great voice from heaven saying unto them, Come up hither. And they went up into heaven in the cloud; and their ene-13 mies beheld them. And in that hour there was a great earthquake, and the tenth part of the city fell; and there were killed in the earthquake seven thousand persons: and the rest were affrighted, and gave glory to the God of heaven.

14 The second Woe is past: behold, the third Woe cometh quickly.

15 And the seventh angel sounded; and there followed great voices in heaven, and they said, The kingdom of the world is become the kingdom of our Lord, and of his Christ: and he shall reign for
16 ever and ever. And the four and twenty elders, which sit before God on their thrones, fell upon their faces, and wor-
17 shipped God, saying, We give thee thanks, O Lord God, the Almighty, which art and which wast; because thou hast taken thy great power, and didst
18 reign. And the nations were wroth, and thy wrath came, and the time of the dead to be judged, and the time to give their reward to thy servants the prophets, and to the saints, and to them that fear thy name, the small and the great; and to destroy them that destroy the earth.

19 And there was opened the temple of God that is in heaven; and there was seen in his temple the ark of his covenant; and there followed lightnings, and voices, and thunders, and an earthquake, and great hail.

12 And a great sign was seen in heaven; a woman arrayed with the sun, and the moon under her feet, and upon her head a crown of twelve stars; and she was
2 with child: and she crieth out, travailing in birth, and in pain to be delivered.
3 And there was seen another sign in heaven; and behold, a great red dragon, having seven heads and ten horns, and
4 upon his heads seven diadems. And his tail draweth the third part of the stars of heaven, and did cast them to the earth: and the dragon stood before the woman which was about to be delivered, that when she was delivered, he
5 might devour her child. And she was delivered of a son, a man child, who is to rule all the nations with a rod of iron:

and her child was caught up unto God,
6 and unto his throne. And the woman fled into the wilderness, where she hath a place prepared of God, that there they may nourish her a thousand two hundred and threescore days.

7 And there was war in heaven: Michael and his angels going forth to war with the dragon; and the dragon warred and
8 his angels; and they prevailed not, neither was their place found any more
9 in heaven. And the great dragon was cast down, the old serpent, he that is called the Devil and Satan, the deceiver of the whole world; he was cast down to the earth, and his angels were cast
10 down with him. And I heard a great voice in heaven, saying, Now is come the salvation, and the power, and the kingdom of our God, and the authority of his Christ: for the accuser of our brethren is cast down, which accuseth them before our God day and night.
11 And they overcame him because of the

blood of the Lamb, and because of the word of their testimony; and they loved 12 not their life even unto death. Therefore rejoice, O heavens, and ye that dwell in them. Woe for the earth and for the sea: because the devil is gone down unto you, having great wrath, knowing that he hath but a short time. 13 And when the dragon saw that he was cast down to the earth, he persecuted the woman which brought forth the man 14 child. And there were given to the woman the two wings of the great eagle, that she might fly into the wilderness unto her place, where she is nourished for a time, and times, and half a time, 15 from the face of the serpent. And the serpent cast out of his mouth after the woman water as a river, that he might cause her to be carried away by the 16 stream. And the earth helped the woman, and the earth opened her mouth, and swallowed up the river which the 17 dragon cast out of his mouth. And the

dragon waxed wroth with the woman, and went away to make war with the rest of her seed, which keep the commandments of God, and hold the testi-
13 mony of Jesus: and he stood upon the sand of the sea.

And I saw a beast coming up out of the sea, having ten horns and seven heads, and on his horns ten diadems, and upon his heads names of blasphemy.
2 And the beast which I saw was like unto a leopard, and his feet were as the feet of a bear, and his mouth as the mouth of a lion: and the dragon gave him his power,
3 and his throne, and great authority. And I saw one of his heads as though it had been smitten unto death; and his death-stroke was healed: and the whole earth
4 wondered after the beast; and they worshipped the dragon, because he gave his authority unto the beast; and they worshipped the beast, saying, Who is like unto the beast? and who is able to war
5 with him? and there was given to him a

mouth speaking great things and blasphemies; and there was given to him authority to continue forty and two
6 months. And he opened his mouth for blasphemies against God, to blaspheme his name, and his tabernacle, even them
7 that dwell in the heaven. And it was given unto him to make war with the saints, and to overcome them: and there was given to him authority over every tribe and people and tongue and nation.
8 And all that dwell on the earth shall worship him, every one whose name hath not been written in the book of life of the Lamb that hath been slain from the foundation of the world. If any man hath an
9 ear, let him hear. If any man is for captivity, into captivity he goeth: if any man shall kill with the sword, with the sword must he be killed. Here is the patience and the faith of the saints.
11 And I saw another beast coming up out of the earth; and he had two horns like unto a lamb, and he spake as a dragon.

12 And he exerciseth all the authority of the
first beast in his sight. And he maketh
the earth and them that dwell therein to
worship the first beast, whose death-stroke
13 was healed. And he doeth great signs,
that he should even make fire to come
down out of heaven upon the earth in
14 the sight of men. And he deceiveth
them that dwell on the earth by reason of
the signs which it was given him to do
in the sight of the beast; saying to them
that dwell on the earth, that they should
make an image to the beast, who hath
15 the stroke of the sword, and lived. And
it was given unto him to give breath to
it, even to the image of the beast, that the
image of the beast should both speak, and
cause that as many as should not worship the image of the beast should be
16 killed. And he causeth all, the small and
the great, and the rich and the poor, and
the free and the bond, that there be given
them a mark on their right hand, or upon
17 their forehead; and that no man should

be able to buy or to sell, save he that hath the mark, even the name of the beast or 18 the number of his name. Here is wisdom. He that hath understanding, let him count the number of the beast; for it is the number of a man: and his number is Six hundred and sixty and six.

14 And I saw, and behold, the Lamb standing on the mount Zion, and with him a hundred and forty and four thousand, having his name, and the name of his Father, written on their foreheads. 2 And I heard a voice from heaven, as the voice of many waters, and as the voice of a great thunder: and the voice which I heard was as the voice of harpers harping 3 with their harps: and they sing as it were a new song before the throne, and before the four living creatures and the elders: and no man could learn the song save the hundred and forty and four thousand, even they that had been purchased out of 4 the earth. These are they which were not defiled with women; for they are

virgins. These are they which follow the Lamb whithersoever he goeth. These were purchased from among men, to be
5 the firstfruits unto the Lamb. And in their mouth was found no lie: they are without blemish.

6 And I saw another angel flying in mid heaven, having an eternal gospel to proclaim unto them that dwell on the earth, and unto every nation and tribe and
7 tongue and people; and he saith with a great voice, Fear God, and give him glory; for the hour of his judgement is come: and worship him that made the heaven and the earth and sea and fountains of waters.

8 And another, a second angel, followed, saying, Fallen, fallen is Babylon the great, which hath made all the nations to drink of the wine of the wrath of her fornication.

9 And another angel, a third, followed them, saying with a great voice, If any man worshippeth the beast and his

image, and receiveth a mark on his forehead, or upon his hand, he also shall drink of the wine of the wrath of God, which is prepared unmixed in the cup of his anger; and he shall be tormented with fire and brimstone in the presence of the holy angels, and in the presence of the Lamb: and the smoke of their torment goeth up for ever and ever; and they have no rest day and night, they that worship the beast and his image, and whoso receiveth the mark of his name.

12 Here is the patience of the saints, they that keep the commandments of God, and the faith of Jesus.

13 And I heard a voice from heaven saying, Write, Blessed are the dead which die in the Lord from henceforth: yea, saith the Spirit, that they may rest from their labours; for their works follow with them.

14 And I saw, and behold, a white cloud; and on the cloud I saw one sitting like unto a son of man, having on his head a golden crown, and in his hand a sharp

15 sickle. And another angel came out from the temple, crying with a great voice to him that sat on the cloud, Send forth thy sickle, and reap: for the hour to reap is come; for the harvest of the earth is
16 overripe. And he that sat on the cloud cast his sickle upon the earth; and the earth was reaped.

17 And another angel came out from the temple which is in heaven, he also having
18 a sharp sickle. And another angel came out from the altar, he that hath power over fire; and he called with a great voice to him that had the sharp sickle, saying, Send forth thy sharp sickle, and gather the clusters of the vine of the earth; for her grapes are fully ripe.
19 And the angel cast his sickle into the earth, and gathered the vintage of the earth, and cast it into the winepress, the great winepress of the wrath of God.
20 And the winepress was trodden without the city, and there came out blood from the winepress, even unto the bridles of the

horses, as far as a thousand and six hundred furlongs.

15 And I saw another sign in heaven, great and marvellous, seven angels having seven plagues, which are the last, for in them is finished the wrath of God.

2 And I saw as it were a glassy sea mingled with fire; and them that come victorious from the beast, and from his image, and from the number of his name, standing by the glassy sea, having harps
3 of God. And they sing the song of Moses the servant of God, and the song of the Lamb, saying, Great and marvellous are thy works, O Lord God, the Almighty; righteous and true are thy
4 ways, thou King of the ages. Who shall not fear, O Lord, and glorify thy name? for thou only art holy; for all the nations shall come and worship before thee; for thy righteous acts have been made manifest.

5 And after these things I saw, and the temple of the tabernacle of the testimony

6 in heaven was opened: and there came out from the temple the seven angels that had the seven plagues, arrayed with precious stone, pure and bright, and girt
7 about their breasts with golden girdles. And one of the four living creatures gave unto the seven angels seven golden bowls full of the wrath of God, who liveth for
8 ever and ever. And the temple was filled with smoke from the glory of God, and from his power; and none was able to enter into the temple, till the seven plagues of the seven angels should be finished.

16 And I heard a great voice out of the temple, saying to the seven angels, Go ye, and pour out the seven bowls of the wrath of God into the earth.
2 And the first went, and poured out his bowl into the earth; and it became a noisome and grievous sore upon the men which had the mark of the beast, and which worshipped his image.
3 And the second poured out his bowl

into the sea; and it became blood as of a dead man; and every living soul died, even the things that were in the sea.

4 And the third poured out his bowl into the rivers and the fountains of the
5 waters; and it became blood. And I heard the angel of the waters saying, Righteous art thou, which art and which wast, thou Holy One, because thou didst
6 thus judge: for they poured out the blood of saints and prophets, and blood hast
7 thou given them to drink: they are worthy. And I heard the altar saying, Yea, O Lord God, the Almighty, true and righteous are thy judgements.

8 And the fourth poured out his bowl upon the sun; and it was given unto it
9 to scorch men with fire. And men were scorched with great heat: and they blasphemed the name of the God which hath the power over these plagues; and they repented not to give him glory.

10 And the fifth poured out his bowl upon the throne of the beast; and his kingdom

was darkened; and they gnawed their
11 tongues for pain, and they blasphemed
the God of heaven because of their pains
and their sores; and they repented not of
their works.

12 And the sixth poured out his bowl
upon the great river, the river Euphrates;
and the water thereof was dried up, that
the way might be made ready for the
13 kings that come from the sunrising.
And I saw coming out of the mouth of
the dragon, and out of the mouth of the
beast, and out of the mouth of the false
prophet, three unclean spirits, as it
14 were frogs: for they are spirits of devils,
working signs; which go forth unto the
kings of the whole world, to gather them
together unto the war of the great day of
15 God, the Almighty. (Behold, I come as
a thief. Blessed is he that watcheth, and
keepeth his garments, lest he walk naked,
16 and they see his shame.) And they
gathered them together into the place
which is called in Hebrew Har-Magedon.

17 And the seventh poured out his bowl upon the air; and there came forth a great voice out of the temple, from the
18 throne, saying, It is done: and there were lightnings, and voices, and thunders; and there was a great earthquake, such as was not since there were men upon the earth,
19 so great an earthquake, so mighty. And the great city was divided into three parts, and the cities of the nations fell: and Babylon the great was remembered in the sight of God, to give unto her the cup of the wine of the fierceness of his
20 wrath. And every island fled away, and
21 the mountains were not found. And great hail, every stone about the weight of a talent, cometh down out of heaven upon men: and men blasphemed God because of the plague of the hail; for the plague thereof is exceeding great.

17 And there came one of the seven angels that had the seven bowls, and spake with me, saying, Come hither, I will shew thee the judgement of the great harlot that

2 sitteth upon many waters; with whom the kings of the earth committed fornication, and they that dwell in the earth were made drunken with the wine of her fornication.
3 And he carried me away in the Spirit into a wilderness: and I saw a woman sitting upon a scarlet-coloured beast, full of names of blasphemy, having
4 seven heads and ten horns. And the woman was arrayed in purple and scarlet, and decked with gold and precious stone and pearls, having in her hand a golden cup full of abominations, even the unclean
5 things of her fornication, and upon her forehead a name written, MYSTERY, BABYLON THE GREAT, THE MOTHER OF THE HARLOTS AND OF THE ABOMINATIONS OF THE EARTH.
6 And I saw the woman drunken with the blood of the saints, and with the blood of the martyrs of Jesus. And when I saw her, I wondered with a great wonder.
7 And the angel said unto me, Wherefore didst thou wonder? I will tell thee the mystery of the woman, and of the beast

that carrieth her, which hath the seven
8 heads and the ten horns. The beast that
thou sawest was, and is not; and is about
to come up out of the abyss, and to go
into perdition. And they that dwell on
the earth shall wonder, they whose name
hath not been written in the book of life
from the foundation of the world, when
they behold the beast, how that he was,
9 and is not, and shall come. Here is the
mind which hath wisdom. The seven
heads are seven mountains, on which the
10 woman sitteth: and they are seven kings;
the five are fallen, the one is, the other is
not yet come; and when he cometh, he
11 must continue a little while. And the
beast that was, and is not, is himself also
an eighth, and is of the seven; and he
12 goeth into perdition. And the ten horns
that thou sawest are ten kings, which have
received no kingdom as yet; but they
receive authority as kings, with the beast,
13 for one hour. These have one mind, and
they give their power and authority unto

14 the beast. These shall war against the Lamb, and the Lamb shall overcome them, for he is Lord of lords, and King of kings; and they also shall overcome that are with him, called and chosen and faith-
15 ful. And he saith unto me, The waters which thou sawest, where the harlot sitteth, are peoples, and multitudes, and
16 nations, and tongues. And the ten horns which thou sawest, and the beast, these shall hate the harlot, and shall make her desolate and naked, and shall eat her flesh, and shall burn her utterly with fire.
17 For God did put in their hearts to do his mind, and to come to one mind, and to give their kingdom unto the beast, until the words of God should be accomplished.
18 And the woman whom thou sawest is the great city, which reigneth over the kings of the earth.
18 After these things I saw another angel coming down out of heaven, having great authority; and the earth was lightened
2 with his glory. And he cried with a

mighty voice, saying, Fallen, fallen is Babylon the great, and is become a habitation of devils, and a hold of every unclean spirit, and a hold of every unclean
3 and hateful bird. For by the wine of the wrath of her fornication all the nations are fallen; and the kings of the earth committed fornication with her, and the merchants of the earth waxed rich by the power of her wantonness.

4 And I heard another voice from heaven, saying, Come forth, my people, out of her, that ye have no fellowship with her sins, and that ye receive not of her
5 plagues: for her sins have reached even unto heaven, and God hath remembered
6 her iniquities. Render unto her even as she rendered, and double unto her the double according to her works: in the cup which she mingled, mingle unto her
7 double. How much soever she glorified herself, and waxed wanton, so much give her of torment and mourning: for she saith in her heart, I sit a queen, and

am no widow, and shall in no wise see
8 mourning. Therefore in one day shall her plagues come, death, and mourning, and famine; and she shall be utterly burned with fire; for strong is the Lord
9 God which judged her. And the kings of the earth, who committed fornication and lived wantonly with her, shall weep and wail over her, when they look upon
10 the smoke of her burning, standing afar off for the fear of her torment, saying, Woe, woe, the great city, Babylon, the strong city! for in one hour is thy judge-
11 ment come. And the merchants of the earth weep and mourn over her, for no man buyeth their merchandise any more;
12 merchandise of gold, and silver, and precious stone, and pearls, and fine linen, and purple, and silk, and scarlet; and all thyine wood, and every vessel of ivory, and every vessel made of most precious wood, and of brass, and iron, and marble;
13 and cinnamon, and spice, and incense, and ointment, and frankincense, and wine,

and oil, and fine flour, and wheat, and cattle, and sheep; and merchandise of horses and chariots and slaves; and souls of men.
14 And the fruits which thy soul lusted after are gone from thee, and all things that were dainty and sumptuous are perished from thee, and men shall find them
15 no more at all. The merchants of these things, who were made rich by her, shall stand afar off for the fear of her torment,
16 weeping and mourning; saying, Woe, woe, the great city, she that was arrayed in fine linen and purple and scarlet, and decked with gold and precious stone and
17 pearl! for in one hour so great riches is made desolate. And every shipmaster, and every one that saileth any whither, and mariners, and as many as gain their
18 living by sea, stood afar off, and cried out as they looked upon the smoke of her burning, saying, What city is like
19 the great city? And they cast dust on their heads, and cried, weeping and mourning, saying, Woe, woe, the great

city, wherein were made rich all that had their ships in the sea by reason of her costliness! for in one hour is she made
20 desolate. Rejoice over her, thou heaven, and ye saints, and ye apostles, and ye prophets; for God hath judged your judgement on her.
21 And a strong angel took up a stone as it were a great millstone, and cast it into the sea, saying, Thus with a mighty fall shall Babylon, the great city, be cast down, and shall be found no more at all.
22 And the voice of harpers and minstrels and flute-players and trumpeters shall be heard no more at all in thee; and no craftsman, of whatsoever craft, shall be found any more at all in thee; and the voice of a millstone shall be heard no
23 more at all in thee; and the light of a lamp shall shine no more at all in thee; and the voice of the bridegroom and of the bride shall be heard no more at all in thee: for thy merchants were the princes of the earth; for with thy sor-

24 cery were all the nations deceived. And in her was found the blood of prophets and of saints, and of all that have been slain upon the earth.

19 After these things I heard as it were a great voice of a great multitude in heaven, saying, Hallelujah; Salvation, and glory,
2 and power, belong to our God: for true and righteous are his judgements; for he hath judged the great harlot, which did corrupt the earth with her fornication, and he hath avenged the blood of his
3 servants at her hand. And a second time they say, Hallelujah. And her
4 smoke goeth up for ever and ever. And the four and twenty elders and the four living creatures fell down and worshipped God that sitteth on the throne, saying,
5 Amen; Hallelujah. And a voice came forth from the throne, saying, Give praise to our God, all ye his servants, ye that
6 fear him, the small and the great. And I heard as it were the voice of a great multitude, and as the voice of many

waters, and as the voice of mighty thunders, saying, Hallelujah: for the Lord
7 our God, the Almighty, reigneth. Let us rejoice and be exceeding glad, and let us give the glory unto him: for the marriage of the Lamb is come, and his wife
8 hath made herself ready. And it was given unto her that she should array herself in fine linen, bright and pure: for the fine linen is the righteous acts of the
9 saints. And he saith unto me, Write, Blessed are they which are bidden to the marriage supper of the Lamb. And he saith unto me, These are true words of
10 God. And I fell down before his feet to worship him. And he saith unto me, See thou do it not: I am a fellow-servant with thee and with thy brethren that hold the testimony of Jesus: worship God: for the testimony of Jesus is the spirit of prophecy.

11 And I saw the heaven opened; and behold, a white horse, and he that sat thereon, called Faithful and True; and

in righteousness he doth judge and make
12 war. And his eyes are a flame of fire, and upon his head are many diadems; and he hath a name written, which no
13 one knoweth but he himself. And he is arrayed in a garment sprinkled with blood: and his name is called The Word
14 of God. And the armies which are in heaven followed him upon white horses, clothed in fine linen, white and pure.
15 And out of his mouth proceedeth a sharp sword, that with it he should smite the nations: and he shall rule them with a rod of iron: and he treadeth the winepress of the fierceness of the wrath of
16 Almighty God. And he hath on his garment and on his thigh a name written, KING OF KINGS, AND LORD OF LORDS.
17 And I saw an angel standing in the sun; and he cried with a loud voice, saying to all the birds that fly in mid heaven, Come and be gathered together
18 unto the great supper of God; that ye may eat the flesh of kings, and the flesh

of captains, and the flesh of mighty men, and the flesh of horses and of them that sit thereon, and the flesh of all men, both free and bond, and small and great.

19 And I saw the beast, and the kings of the earth, and their armies, gathered together to make war against him that sat upon the horse, and against his army.

20 And the beast was taken, and with him the false prophet that wrought the signs in his sight, wherewith he deceived them that had received the mark of the beast, and them that worshipped his image: they twain were cast alive into the lake

21 of fire that burneth with brimstone: and the rest were killed with the sword of him that sat upon the horse, even the sword which came forth out of his mouth: and all the birds were filled with their flesh.

20 And I saw an angel coming down out of heaven, having the key of the abyss

2 and a great chain in his hand. And he laid hold on the dragon, the old serpent,

which is the Devil and Satan, and bound
3 him for a thousand years, and cast him
into the abyss, and shut it, and sealed it
over him, that he should deceive the nations no more, until the thousand years
should be finished: after this he must be
loosed for a little time.

4 And I saw thrones, and they sat upon
them, and judgement was given unto
them: and I saw the souls of them that
had been beheaded for the testimony of
Jesus, and for the word of God, and such
as worshipped not the beast, neither his
image, and received not the mark upon
their forehead and upon their hand; and
they lived, and reigned with Christ a
5 thousand years. The rest of the dead
lived not until the thousand years should
be finished. This is the first resurrection.
6 Blessed and holy is he that hath part
in the first resurrection: over these the
second death hath no power; but they
shall be priests of God and of Christ, and
shall reign with him a thousand years.

7 And when the thousand years are finished, Satan shall be loosed out of his
8 prison, and shall come forth to deceive the nations which are in the four corners of the earth, Gog and Magog, to gather them together to the war: the number
9 of whom is as the sand of the sea. And they went up over the breadth of the earth, and compassed the camp of the saints about, and the beloved city: and fire came down out of heaven, and de-
10 voured them. And the devil that deceived them was cast into the lake of fire and brimstone, where are also the beast and the false prophet; and they shall be tormented day and night for ever and ever.
11 And I saw a great white throne, and him that sat upon it, from whose face the earth and the heaven fled away; and
12 there was found no place for them. And I saw the dead, the great and the small, standing before the throne; and books were opened: and another book was

opened, which is the book of life: and the dead were judged out of the things which were written in the books, according to
13 their works. And the sea gave up the dead which were in it; and death and Hades gave up the dead which were in them: and they were judged every man
14 according to their works. And death and Hades were cast into the lake of fire. This is the second death, even the lake
15 of fire. And if any was not found written in the book of life, he was cast into the lake of fire.

21 And I saw a new heaven and a new earth: for the first heaven and the first earth are passed away; and the sea is
2 no more. And I saw the holy city, new Jerusalem, coming down out of heaven from God, made ready as a bride adorned
3 for her husband. And I heard a great voice out of the throne saying, Behold, the tabernacle of God is with men, and he shall dwell with them, and they shall be his peoples, and God himself shall

4 be with them, and be their God: and he shall wipe away every tear from their eyes; and death shall be no more; neither shall there be mourning, nor crying, nor pain, any more: the first things
5 are passed away. And he that sitteth on the throne said, Behold, I make all things new. And he saith, Write: for
6 these words are faithful and true. And he said unto me, They are come to pass. I am the Alpha and the Omega, the beginning and the end. I will give unto him that is athirst of the fountain of the
7 water of life freely. He that overcometh shall inherit these things; and I will be
8 his God, and he shall be my son. But for the fearful, and unbelieving, and abominable, and murderers, and fornicators, and sorcerers, and idolaters, and all liars, their part shall be in the lake that burneth with fire and brimstone; which is the second death.
9 And there came one of the seven angels who had the seven bowls, who were laden

with the seven last plagues; and he spake with me, saying, Come hither, I will shew thee the bride, the wife of the
10 Lamb. And he carried me away in the Spirit to a mountain great and high, and shewed me the holy city Jerusalem, coming down out of heaven from God, having
11 the glory of God: her light was like unto a stone most precious, as it were a jasper
12 stone, clear as crystal: having a wall great and high; having twelve gates, and at the gates twelve angels; and names written thereon, which are the names of the twelve tribes of the children of Israel:
13 on the east were three gates; and on the north three gates; and on the south three
14 gates; and on the west three gates. And the wall of the city had twelve foundations, and on them twelve names of the
15 twelve apostles of the Lamb. And he that spake with me had for a measure a golden reed to measure the city, and the
16 gates thereof, and the wall thereof. And the city lieth foursquare, and the length

thereof is as great as the breadth: and he measured the city with the reed, twelve thousand furlongs: the length and the breadth and the height thereof 17 are equal. And he measured the wall thereof, a hundred and forty and four cubits, according to the measure of a man, 18 that is, of an angel. And the building of the wall thereof was jasper: and the city 19 was pure gold, like unto pure glass. The foundations of the wall of the city were adorned with all manner of precious stones. The first foundation was jasper; the second, sapphire; the third, chalced- 20 ony; the fourth, emerald; the fifth, sardonyx; the sixth, sardius; the seventh, chrysolite; the eighth, beryl; the ninth, topaz; the tenth, chrysoprase; the eleventh, jacinth; the twelfth, amethyst. 21 And the twelve gates were twelve pearls; each one of the several gates was of one pearl: and the street of the city was pure 22 gold, as it were transparent glass. And I saw no temple therein: for the Lord

God the Almighty, and the Lamb, are the
23 temple thereof. And the city hath no
need of the sun, neither of the moon, to
shine upon it: for the glory of God did
lighten it, and the lamp thereof is the
24 Lamb. And the nations shall walk
amidst the light thereof: and the kings
of the earth do bring their glory into it.
25 And the gates thereof shall in no wise be
shut by day (for there shall be no night
26 there): and they shall bring the glory
and the honour of the nations into it:
27 and there shall in no wise enter into it
any thing unclean, or he that maketh an
abomination and a lie: but only they
which are written in the Lamb's book of
22 life. And he shewed me a river of water
of life, bright as crystal, proceeding out of
2 the throne of God and of the Lamb, in
the midst of the street thereof. And on
this side of the river and on that was the
tree of life, bearing twelve manner of
fruits, yielding its fruit every month: and
the leaves of the tree were for the healing

3 of the nations. And there shall be no curse any more: and the throne of God and of the Lamb shall be therein: and
4 his servants shall do him service; and they shall see his face; and his name
5 shall be on their foreheads. And there shall be night no more; and they need no light of lamp, neither light of sun; for the Lord God shall give them light: and they shall reign for ever and ever.
6 And he said unto me, These words are faithful and true: and the Lord, the God of the spirits of the prophets, sent his angel to shew unto his servants the things
7 which must shortly come to pass. And behold, I come quickly. Blessed is he that keepeth the words of the prophecy of this book.
8 And I John am he that heard and saw these things. And when I heard and saw, I fell down to worship before the feet of the angel which shewed me these things.
9 And he saith unto me, See thou do it

not: I am a fellow-servant with thee and with thy brethren the prophets, and with them which keep the words of this book: worship God.

10 And he saith unto me, Seal not up the words of the prophecy of this book; for
11 the time is at hand. He that is unrighteous, let him do unrighteousness still: and he that is filthy, let him be made filthy still: and he that is righteous, let him do righteousness still: and he that is
12 holy, let him be made holy still. Behold, I come quickly; and my reward is with me, to render to each man according as his
13 work is. I am the Alpha and the Omega, the first and the last, the beginning and
14 the end. Blessed are they that wash their robes, that they may have the right to come to the tree of life, and may enter
15 in by the gates into the city. Without are the dogs, and the sorcerers, and the fornicators, and the murderers, and the idolaters, and every one that loveth and maketh a lie.

16 I Jesus have sent mine angel to testify unto you these things for the churches. I am the root and the offspring of David, the bright, the morning star.

17 And the Spirit and the bride say, Come. And he that heareth, let him say, Come. And he that is athirst, let him come: he that will, let him take the water of life freely.

18 I testify unto every man that heareth the words of the prophecy of this book, if any man shall add unto them, God shall add unto him the plagues which
19 are written in this book: and if any man shall take away from the words of the book of this prophecy, God shall take away his part from the tree of life, and out of the holy city, which are written in this book.

20 He which testifieth these things saith, Yea: I come quickly. Amen: come, Lord Jesus.

21 The grace of the Lord Jesus be with the saints. Amen.

APPENDIX

The following table of the Acts and Scenes of the drama is arranged with reference to the scheme here adopted. Together with this are given the corresponding passages in the Book of the Revelation, where they may be found, and the pages of this Essay on which they are mentioned.

Title,	Chap.	I, 1–4.	Page	35
Prologue,	"	I, 4–II.	"	35
Salutation,	"	II–IV.	"	38

ACT I. THE OPENING OF THE SEALS OF FATE

	Chap. IV–VIII, 2.	Page 38–48
Scene 1,	" IV.	" 38
" 2,	" V.	" 43
" 3,	" VI.	" 44
" 4,	" VII–VIII, 2.	" 45

ACT II. THE BLOWING OF THE TRUMPETS OF WOE

	Chap. VIII, 2–XII.	Page 48–57
Scene 1,	" VIII, 2–6.	" 48
" 2,	" VIII, 6–X.	" 49
" 3,	" X.	" 52
" 4,	" XI, 1–15.	" 53
" 5,	" XI, 15–XII.	" 56

ACT III. THE ESTABLISHMENT OF THE KINGDOM, AND
ITS RESULTS

	Chap.	XII–XV.	Page	57-69
Scene 1,	"	XII.	"	57
" 2,	"	XIII.	"	59
" 3,	"	XIV.	"	63

ACT IV. THE JUDGMENT OF THE EARTH AND OF ROME

	Chap.	XV–XIX, 5.	Page	69-76
Scene 1,	"	XV, 1-5.	"	69
" 2,	"	XV, 5-XVII.	"	70
" 3,	"	XVII, XVIII.	"	72
" 4,	"	XIX, 1-5.	"	75

ACT V. THE MARRIAGE OF THE PRINCE OF HEAVEN,
AND THE GLORY OF THE KINGDOM

	Chap.	XIX, 5–XXII, 6.	Page	76-85
Scene 1,	"	XIX, 5–XX.	"	76
" 2,	"	XX.	"	77
" 3,	"	XXI–XXII, 6.	"	80

| Epilogue, | Chap. | XXII, 6-18. | Page | 85 |
| Envoi, | " | XXII, 18–. | " | 86 |

New Testament Handbooks

EDITED BY

SHAILER MATHEWS

*Professor of New Testament History and Interpretation,
University of Chicago*

Arrangements are made for the following volumes, and the publishers will, on request, send notice of the issue of each volume as it appears and each descriptive circular sent out later; such requests for information should state whether address is permanent or not: —

The History of the Textual Criticism of the New Testament

Prof. MARVIN R. VINCENT, Professor of New Testament Exegesis, Union Theological Seminary. [*Now ready.*

Professor Vincent's contributions to the study of the New Testament rank him among the first American exegetes. His most recent publication is "A Critical and Exegetical Commentary on the Epistles to the Philippians and to Philemon" (*International Critical Commentary*), which was preceded by a "Students' New Testament Handbook," "Word Studies in the New Testament," and others.

The History of the Higher Criticism of the New Testament

Prof. HENRY S. NASH, Professor of New Testament Interpretation, Cambridge Divinity School. [*Now ready.*

Of Professor Nash's "Genesis of the Social Conscience," *The Outlook* said: "The results of Professor Nash's ripe thought are presented in a luminous, compact, and often epigrammatic style. The treatment is at once masterful and helpful, and the book ought to be a quickening influence of the highest kind; it surely will establish the fame of its author as a profound thinker, one from whom we have a right to expect future inspiration of a kindred sort."

Introduction to the Books of the New Testament

Prof. B. WISNER BACON, Professor of New Testament Interpretation, Yale University. [*Now ready.*

Professor Bacon's works in the field of Old Testament criticism include "The Triple Tradition of Exodus," and "The Genesis of Genesis," a study of the documentary sources of the books of Moses. In the field of New Testament study he has published a number of brilliant papers, the most recent of which is "The Autobiography of Jesus," in the *American Journal of Theology*.

The History of New Testament Times in Palestine

Prof. SHAILER MATHEWS, Professor of New Testament History and Interpretation, The University of Chicago. [*Now ready.*

The Congregationalist says of Prof. Shailer Mathews's recent work, "The Social Teaching of Jesus": "Re-reading deepens the impression that the author is scholarly, devout, awake to all modern thought, and yet conservative and pre-eminently sane. If, after reading the chapters dealing with Jesus' attitude toward man, society, the family, the state, and wealth, the reader will not agree with us in this opinion, we greatly err as prophets."

The Life of Paul

Prof. RUSH RHEES, President of the University of Rochester.

Professor Rhees is well known from his series of "Inductive Lessons" contributed to the *Sunday School Times*. His "Outline of the Life of Paul," privately printed, has had a flattering reception from New Testament scholars.

The History of the Apostolic Age

Dr. C. W. VOTAW, Instructor in New Testament Literature, The University of Chicago.

Of Dr. Votaw's "Inductive Study of the Founding of the Christian Church," *Modern Church*, Edinburgh, says: "No fuller analysis of the later books of the New Testament could be desired, and no better programme could be offered for their study, than that afforded in the scheme of fifty lessons on the *Founding of the Christian Church*, by Clyde W. Votaw. It is well adapted alike for practical and more scholarly students of the Bible."

The Teaching of Jesus

Prof. GEORGE B. STEVENS, Professor of Systematic Theology, Yale University. [*Now ready*.

Professor Stevens's volumes upon "The Johannine Theology," "The Pauline Theology," as well as his recent volume on "The Theology of the New Testament," have made him probably the most prominent writer on biblical theology in America. His new volume will be among the most important of his works.

The Biblical Theology of the New Testament

Prof. E. P. GOULD, Professor of New Testament Interpretation, Protestant Episcopal Divinity School, Philadelphia. [*Now ready*.

Professor Gould's Commentaries on the Gospel of Mark (in the *International Critical Commentary*) and the Epistles to the Corinthians (in the *American Commentary*) are critical and exegetical attempts to supply those elements which are lacking in existing works of the same general aim and scope.

The History of Christian Literature until Eusebius

Prof. J. W. PLATNER, Professor of Early Church History, Harvard University.

Professor Platner's work will not only treat the writings of the early Christian writers, but will also treat of the history of the New Testament Canon.

OTHERS TO FOLLOW

"An excellent series of scholarly, yet concise and inexpensive New Testament handbooks." — *Christian Advocate*, New York.

"These books are remarkably well suited in language, style, and price, to all students of the New Testament." — *The Congregationalist*, Boston.

THE MACMILLAN COMPANY

66 FIFTH AVENUE, NEW YORK